RAMPAL AND HIS FAMILY

URSULA SHARMA

RAMPAL AND HIS FAMILY

COLLINS
St James's Place, London
1971

William Collins Sons & Co Ltd
London · Glasgow · Sydney · Auckland
Toronto · Johannesburg

First published 1971
© Ursula Sharma
ISBN 0 00 211722 3
Set in Monotype Garamond
Made and Printed in Great Britain by
William Collins Sons & Co Ltd Glasgow

TO MY MOTHER

Acknowledgements

Many of my friends have helped me by discussing the material in this book with me and by giving me their suggestions and comments, and I am very grateful to them. In particular I should like to mention Miss K. Bhalla and Mrs. Ahalya Sharma and to thank them for their assistance. I should also like to acknowledge my debt to my husband, Mr. Om Prakash Sharma, for all the help he gave me in recording and translating the conversations on which this book is based.

Contents

7

CONTENTS

Part 3

SATYA'S STORY

CONTENTS

Part 4

ASHA HAS SOMETHING TO SAY

Part One

INTRODUCTION

*

Introduction

RAMPAL'S house is not shy. It distinguishes itself from the rest of the drab terrace of Edwardian villas with an unselfconscious display of red-painted brickwork and gay yellow window frames. Rampal bought this house two years ago, four years after he arrived in London from India, and he is very proud of it.

A Hindu god smiles down benignly from a brightly coloured print pinned above the front door. I ring the bell. Cautiously the door opens, and it is Asha who is opening it. Her hair hangs half plaited and half loose, for she has just had her bath and her mother has not yet finished doing her hair. Satya and Rampal are delighted to receive a Sunday visitor, and welcome me in.

The front room tries to be splendid, but fails through being too much lived in. The walls are covered in shiny gold paper and the curtains are of heavy brocade, but the sofa is littered with clothes, toys are scattered on the floor and the baby's bottle is lying on one of the chairs. On the mantelpiece are several framed prints of assorted Hindu deities and Sikh saints. There is even a small picture of the Virgin and Child amidst this catholic jumble.

Satya is squatting on the floor, ironing the children's clothes. She is short and plump, bright and motherly. She might be in her late thirties. Her face is attractive and intelligent, her eyes gay and beautiful. She wears the Punjabi *salvar-kamiz* – a loose dress over baggy trousers, with a scarf thrown across the shoulders. Rampal is a slight, rather tense-looking man who looks neither quite young nor quite middle-aged. His face seems both worried and alert. He is sitting cross-legged on the sofa, rocking the baby (a little boy of about two years old) to sleep in his lap.

Satya tells Asha to put the kettle on and while the little girl is making the tea she relates to us all the little incidents which have distinguished her week, details of home and factory life. Asha appears, half-hidden by a tray loaded with tea things and plates of sweets, made by Satya the same morning.

'Now you tell us something new,' says Satya and she leans forward, eager for conversation.

Asha watches us while we chat. She is eight years old, quiet and observant. She is the kind of child whose very quietness sometimes tempts adults to reveal more than they may have wished to her listening ears, unaware that she misses nothing. Her elder brother and sister are in the back room, watching television. Sarinder is a good-natured, talkative thirteen-year-old, who genially admits that his teacher at school calls him a chatter-box. The eldest child, Pritam, is nearly sixteen but looks younger than her age. Much childhood illness and glandular trouble have left her weak and backward. But she is a merry girl, affectionate and sociable. The children, unlike their parents, speak to each other as often in English as in Punjabi, their own language. Even the baby, Pappi, who admittedly was born in London, knows as many English words as he does Punjabi. Their chatter is little understood by Satya and Rampal, whose English remains halting and limited.

The Sunday afternoon passes quietly. Satya begins to prepare the evening meal of *chapatties*, curried vegetables and lentils, served with a lemon pickle of her own making. Rampal is busy laying the new linoleum (which he bought a week ago) in the hall and passage.

I take my leave early, for Rampal and Satya generally go to bed soon after ten. Satya works in a factory, Rampal as an electrician for the Ministry of Works, and both have to be at work early the next morning. Satya stands at the threshold, watching me walk back to the station down the quiet streets of the West London suburb.

* * *

14

This book is the story of Rampal and Satya, of how they emigrated from the peasant villages, first to live in the city of Delhi and later to *vilayat*. *Vilayat* (origin of the word 'Blighty') is used by the Indian peasant to mean 'abroad', but especially England, and as he will tell you, *vilayat* is a land which is far away and very rich, a kind of peasant Eldorado.

No one can tell the tale better than Rampal and Satya themselves, and therefore the words in this book are their own, taken down in a series of tape-recording sessions during visits of the kind I have described.

Their story is dramatic enough and entertaining in its own right, but this was not my main reason for writing it down. The coming of large numbers of immigrants from India and Pakistan to English industrial cities has brought about a confrontation between peoples whose skin colour is only the most superficial of their differences. Most of these immigrants – Muslims from Pakistan, Sikhs and Hindus from India – come from rural areas of the Punjab, from village communities where attitudes towards such matters as marriage, sex, parent-child relationships and social hierarchy are very different from those held by the English people amongst whom these newcomers settle. The immigrant does not suddenly spring into existence when he arrives at an English airport. If he is an adult, he comes having already formed his values and his expectations from society in a very different environment, many thousands of miles away. He cannot be expected to adjust overnight on arrival here.

If, as is often the case, his English is very limited, then it will be hard enough for him to discover what kind of behaviour is expected of him, let alone to conform to this pattern straightaway.

These differences in attitude between host and immigrant have often been the immediate causes of misunderstandings between them. A Sikh bus conductor is threatened with dismissal if he does not remove his turban; a Punjabi father is unwilling to send his teen-age daughter to school in a dress which exposes her legs; English ambulance men refuse to remove their shoes before entering a Sikh temple to attend to a member of the congregation who has fallen ill. I emphasise that these failures to understand the social values of others are only the immediate causes of tension between communities for I recognise that there are almost always others, economic (such as housing shortages or fear of unemployment) or psychological (such as the prejudice which springs more from a certain kind of personality structure than from any objective conditions). These are far harder to remedy, of course. But if more were known about the values and attitudes which the immigrant brings with him it might help to avert incidents which exacerbate existing tension, as well as assist the newcomer to adjust to a strange environment. Rampal and Satya can tell us something about this and it is with this in mind that I have included so much of what they have to say about their childhood and upbringing. The early chapters in their stories tell us about the environment in which they matured the emotional and moral resources which they bring to bear upon their experiences in London. The kind of society in which they grew up can be compared with the environment in which their more Anglicised children are spending their formative years, and the difference between the two will suggest the kind of tensions which may be expected to arise between the two generations later (and which are no doubt already being felt in immigrant families where the children are older). Asha, Sarinder and Pritam seem Indian enough at home, but outside it (and even with each other) they speak English with the local accent; they read comics, watch television, and are generally exposed to most of the influences to which English boys and girls of their age are also exposed, and from which their parents are excluded, mainly because of their poor understanding of the English language.

In this book I have also tried to demonstrate a way of seeing the situation from the immigrant's own point of view. A more friendly attitude towards the immigrant might well be cultivated if we were only more aware of what it is like to be in his position. Putting ourselves in the immigrant's shoes, learning how the environment which seems ordinary and un-problematic to us may appear hostile and confusing to him, is a good exercise in overcoming the sense of otherness which divides us from him. Rampal's and Satya's stories show us the immigrant's world from within; we see ourselves as others see us.

I have arranged the material in this book in the form of two life histories, first Rampal's and then Satya's. Being subjective, this material is bound to be highly personal. It would be ridiculous to suggest that all Indian immigrants have exactly the same experiences and opinions as these two. Many coloured immigrants might feel, for instance, that Satya underestimates the amount of colour prejudice which exists in Britain, or that Rampal's sense of isolation is more pronounced than their own. Satya and Rampal themselves differ markedly from each other in their reactions to certain events and ideas. For instance, Rampal feels that he has been poor all his life, whilst Satya feels that she had always enjoyed a satisfactory standard of living.[1] But there is also much in their experiences and attitudes which is fairly general amongst Indian immigrants and which echoes the findings of researchers such as, for instance, R. Desai.[2] There is their lack of informal social contact with English people, the persistence of patterns of behaviour learnt in India (such as the buying of jewellery as an investment or the giving of large dowries at marriage). Rampal's story of his misguided expectations about the easy time and the wealth he would have in England cannot be unusual, and his view of English sexual mores is quite a common one amongst Indian immigrants.

Being a sociologist, I am beset with the temptation to

1. Sometimes Satya or Rampal expresses different feelings about the same subject on separate occasions, but I have tried to resist the temptation to iron out these inconsistencies in order to prevent a 'tidy' account. After all, few people have simple straightforward feelings about the things which concern them closely. Our deepest emotions are often the most complex and ambivalent.

2. R. Desai. *Indian Immigrants in Britain.* Oxford University Press, 1963.

abstract further generalisations from this material and to add much sociological comment of my own. But I will resist it firmly, for I believe that these stories speak for themselves. I should, however, add more to explain the method used in recording and compiling them. The tape recorder is being used as an aid to research by an increasing number of social scientists and writers. Oscar Lewis has used the tape recorded life history method in his study of urban poverty in Mexico[1] and Tony Parker has used a similar technique in his study of the making of a criminal.[2] This method requires a very confident and even intimate relationship between the investigator and his subject. The researcher must be both humane and discreet, not in any way exploiting his subject's confidence. He must neither patronise nor deceive. I hope, therefore, that I have not offended against my friends nor misrepresented them in any way, and I beg their forgiveness if they feel that I have done so.

Several reasons led me to choose this particular family to study.[3] Rampal and Satya are fairly typical Indian immigrants in important respects; they come from a rural background, have a young family, work in manual jobs, are not highly educated. And in case I am criticised by more educated Indians for selecting such a family, let me emphasise that I deliberately avoided choosing a 'middle-class' family, even though there are large numbers of educated professional Indians living in England also, because I felt that the more westernised immigrant did not have the same difficulty in communication. The Rampals and Satyas of London are articulate in their own tongue but know little English, and are therefore dumb to the English public.

I explained the aim of the project to Satya and Rampal and they entered into it willingly and with enthusiasm. They needed little questioning or prompting during our recording sessions:

1. Oscar Lewis. *The Children of Sanchez*. Penguin Modern Classics, 1964.
2. Tony Parker. *The Courage of his Convictions*. Hutchinson, 1962.
3. I have, of course, used pseudonyms and omitted place names and references such as might reveal their identity.

I generally found that a single leading question would elicit as much as thirty or forty minutes of free reflection and recollection. Just as Oscar Lewis found that his Mexican subjects seemed to experience a sense of catharsis in relating their life stories, so I also had the impression that Rampal and Satya too derived some relief from this unburdening of their feelings and experiences. The sessions were informal and enjoyable. Punjabis are often good raconteurs, perhaps the uneducated men and women of the villages especially so. Individuals who are as articulate as Rampal and Satya are in no way unusual. Telling folk tales and recounting witty anecdotes are important forms of amusement in the rural villages where there are no cinemas, magazines, television, or the many other forms of mass entertainment that we take for granted. A witty story teller or a convincing speaker is generally admired.

These stories needed very little editing or re-arranging, but I have retained some Punjabi terms where this seemed appropriate, explaining them in a separate glossary. Asha's epilogue was recorded in English and I have not altered her words. The rhythm of her parents' rustic Punjabi is difficult to reproduce in translation but I have done my best to reflect some of the colour and vigour of their speech.

It remains only for me to express my gratitude to Rampal and Satya for their hospitality, so often and so generously given, my pleasure in their sincere and unaffected friendship, and my hope that its fruits, in the form of this book, may contribute something to the mutual understanding of English and Indian people in the future.[1]

1. The recent report on British race relations, *Colour and Citizenship*, published in 1969 by the Oxford University Press, is recommended to those who are interested in a more comprehensive study of the situation. It contains specific sections concerning Indian immigrants, and a useful bibliography.

Part Two

RAMPAL'S STORY

*

Chapter 1

THE MONEY-LENDER'S SON

I WAS born in poverty and spent my youth in poverty. Every child that is born has its own apportioned fate; some are born into ease and joy, others into trouble and suffering, some to inherit riches or land, others to inherit only poverty. Some children when they are born bring good fortune with them; they live to serve their parents all their life, and with their coming the whole family flourishes and becomes rich. Others bring only misfortune and misery, even death, with them. Our little Pappi must have a happy fate, for since his birth God has been good to us and resolved all our difficulties; now we have money, work, our own house, and we live contentedly. But when I was born my coming was not so fortunate. Before I was ten years old my father had lost all his wealth. We cannot say why these things happen, only that they do happen. Ordinary men who are neither gods nor saints might not be capable of understanding, even if they were to be told. But certainly it must be according to what we have deserved in former births that God decides in what circumstances we are to be born.

My father had not always been poor. My elder brother, Jagdish, was seventeen years my senior and my sister twelve years older than myself, and when they were born my parents had been prosperous. My father was a money-lender in our village and made a profit from lending and receiving. Those were years of wealth and he was able to educate his first two children and do much for them. And even in my early years we were not so badly off. But when I was ten my elder brother lost Rs. 10,000 of my father's money speculating on the corn market. After that our whole family's fortunes began to sink, with the result that neither I nor my younger brother were able to complete our education, for our father could not afford our school fees. He was even obliged to sell one of the two houses we owned; my forefathers had originally lived in a small town nearby and it was my grandfather who had come to settle in the village where I was brought up. Poverty eventually forced my father to dispose of the house we owned in the place our ancestors had come from.

My father commanded great respect in the village where we lived. All the villagers looked up to him. And well they might; people in the villages are poor and poverty draws one man to another. When a man is in need, his need takes him straight to the money-lender. 'Misfortune has befallen me. I am in need of money,' he says – and if he receives the sum he asks for he is bound to the money-lender by his obligation. In the village it often happens like this, that a farmer's work is going well on all sides – everything he turns his hand to seems to yield gold and he becomes over-confident. 'No one is half as clever as I am,' he thinks, 'for everything I do prospers.' So he buys more land and rents it out to tenants. But then his problems start, because the trouble with land owning is that you must pay the land tax to the government. So suppose the crop is poor, the land is not as fertile as he had thought, or suppose the tenant refuses to pay his rent – then the farmer is obliged to run to the money-lender to raise the sum he needs. What seems easy and desirable from afar is full of problems when you are in the midst of it. It is as though a man seeing a date palm from a distance thinks, 'Come along, let us climb up and have some dates. The tree is tall, to be sure, but never mind; we shall get up somehow or other.' Only when he is stuck half-way up and is unable to climb farther or come down does he realise what a difficult task he has undertaken. He cannot move forward yet when he looks down at the drop beneath him his hands shake with fright and he has to call for help. The farmer's life is like that too. It looks easy enough to others but those who experience it find out all its trials and difficulties. It was these difficulties which would bring villagers to my father to seek loans. I can even remember a man being so desperate for money that he came to my father at night when he was asleep.

He woke him by gently shaking his feet. My father immediately woke up and said, 'Brother, what have you come for at this time?' The man explained that he needed a sum of money urgently to pay for his son's wedding and of course Pitaji made him over the amount he needed there and then.

Chapter 2

A PUNJABI VILLAGE

LET me describe to you the village where I was born and spent my childhood. Each family in the village had its own courtyard and their dwelling quarters and outhouses would be built facing on to this enclosure. The houses were constructed from bricks made out of baked clay and about two thirds of them were *pakka*,[1] the remainder were *kaccha*. Each house, or *haveli*, had at least three rooms. One would be a byre for the cattle and there would be pegs set in the floor for tethering the beasts, for they were always brought indoors during the monsoon storms. You could not leave animals outside in such torrential rain. Then there would be another room where the fodder for the cattle was kept; chaff and straw would be stored there after the harvests to feed the beasts during the winter. The third room would provide living quarters for the family. They would sleep there at nights and there would be plenty of space for guests also. Some houses had more rooms – after all it was no cramped city that we lived in. There was no shortage of space and each family could find room to build on additions to their house if they wished it. The villager may not be rich but his house is a palace compared with the crowded tenement the townsman knows. Some of the houses in our village were set in an acre or more of enclosed land.

If I were to take you round our village I could point out each

1. See glossary at p. 217.

house and tell you who lived there. Here is so-and-so's house, here is so-and-so's courtyard. All the wells in the village were named – the Well by the Gate, Hari Ram's Well, Gurmukh Singh's Well. Here is the store kept by the Brahmans and here is the Chimba's shop. Here we have the mill where the farmers grind their corn and wheat to make flour. Over there is the *divankhana*, and on this side is the *dharamsala*, the rest-house where pilgrims and travellers can get a night's shelter. And here by the gate of the *dharamsala* is the place where the Bharvale make their fires. The Bharvale were a special caste whose task it was to maintain fires in the village. In the days when I was a child, matches were still a rare luxury for ordinary villagers and it was necessary that someone in the village should keep a fire going all the time so that anyone could get a light if their own fire went out. I don't think that there are any Bharvale left in the village now; since Pakistan was created in 1947 they have all left. But in those days it was their task to see that there was always a light available in the village. Each day they would collect all the fuel they could, picking up dried cow-dung, sticks, anything that would burn, from the paths and by-ways, then gathering it together in one place. Early each morning they would replenish the fires they kept burning from this stock of fuel so that they never went out. During the day they would take embers round to any house where there was need of a light. Each household would give them a portion of grain at harvest time as payment for this service.

At each entrance to the village there were gates and only through them could we go in and out. In the days of Muslim rule,[1] so our Pitaji used to explain to us, the villages would be assaulted by bands of raiders. It was villages like ours, lying on the main routes between Delhi and Lahore, which were most open to the attacks of invading armies. Sometimes it would be

1. During mediaeval times the Punjab was ruled by various Muslim dynasties. Muslim rule was brought to an end when the rising power of the Sikhs brought about the collapse of Mogul authority in the Punjab in the eighteenth century. Sikh rule ended when the British annexed the Punjab in 1849.

one village's turn, sometimes another's, and it continued like
that during the years of Sikh rule also. The villages were always
liable to be raided for valuables. It did not matter whether the
village was a rich one with big *pakka* houses or only a mean
hamlet with *kaccha* huts, for it was not just money the raiders
were after. They were after food also and they would not leave
a village until they had looted all the grain which the farmers
had set by. Yet according to my father, the villagers often met
the raiders with affection rather than fear. They would tell
them, 'Stay with us and we will build you houses and byres;
stay with us so that we will be strong in numbers. Then who
will dare attack us in future?' They would rather join their
attackers to themselves in order to increase their strength and
the population of their settlement. In those days men were
generous and even though the wheat they had was little enough
they would share it with the new settlers. The newcomers
would then either rent land from them, or more often rear
cattle and live by selling their milk and butter to the others.
That is how life was in those days.

Even in my own life I have been the onlooker of so many
changes taking place in the countryside. Nowadays so many
machines are made for every purpose. For example, there are
harvesting machines which cut the stalks of the corn and jute
to within a few inches of the ground. With the old methods,
stalks a foot or so in length would be left in the fields and the
poor people would come gleaning after the reaping was done.
There were gleanings to be had in plenty and after the threshing there was chaff to be collected, fodder for the cattle. Now
everything is sucked up into the machines and this useful
waste is no longer there for poor people to help themselves to.
In those days – when I was a boy – the poor were pinched for
cash sure enough; they had no pennies in their pockets. But
there was an abundance of good things freely available. In
these days – especially since Independence – things are exactly
the reverse. Life is made of money now. The villager will sell
his crop for cash but everything is so costly. What will he do
even if he manages to sell every ear of wheat? When all the

things in the shops are so dear that the peasant can never afford to buy them, what pleasure will he derive from just looking at them and knowing that they can never be his? Now all trans-actions are done with money whereas, before, people would exchange the things they had excess of for the things they lacked. With such giving went affection and generous feelings, but cash is no substitute for affection. Moreover, affection thrives when you can say without hesitation to anyone who passes your door, 'Come in, sit down and take your meal with us.' When there is nothing in the grain bin, affection is harder to nourish.

When I was young I used to take pleasure in the simple good nature of my village friends. Here and there you would come across a devious fellow but the majority were straightforward men. If anyone borrowed from my father and later denied that he had ever had it, there was always one sure way to get him to come out with the truth. In those days people had such re-spect for the things they held sacred – the cow, the *pipal* tree, the holy Ganges, that they would never tell a lie when they swore by these things. Nowadays, not only will they perjure themselves with one hand laid on the cow's tail, they will even eat the poor beast's flesh as well. That is why I say that for me village life has become spoilt now. Modern life has corrupted that innocent simplicity, and I feel no desire to go back there to live. When I was a child, the village was not such a comfort-able place to live but there was more warmth in the life people led there. Now if you were to see our village you would say that it is a fine place in appearance, with so many modern devices to make life comfortable – machines, electricity, trans-port – but I tell you there is not a straw's worth of humanity in the life of the place.

Chapter 3

PARENTS AND SONS

MY parents were not overstrict with us and never nagged us saying, 'Don't do this, don't do that.' Indeed, I remember that it was my elder brother who was always telling me off for smoking cigarettes when I was a lad, not my father. (Mind you I still went on smoking them on the sly.) Perhaps my parents realised that you can only tell what is right and wrong from your own experience in the end. Everyone learns from what he sees with his own eyes and will not heed another's warning.

I think that I was closer to my mother than to my father. My father was one kind of person, my mother was quite another. When my father lost all his money he was a broken man. You could say that he was much more involved in his money than my mother was, and hence he suffered greater disappointment and bitterness at that time. My mother was less disturbed. Let riches come or go, she was only concerned with her children. When I grew up and joined the army during the war-time, I used to send money home in her name. But when the postman brought her the money order for Rs. 15 each month she would not touch it. She would just make her thumb print on the receipt (she was illiterate and so could not sign her name) and then say to my father, 'There, if you want money, take it. What use is it to me? I only want to see my son again.' She loved me so much that her sight grew dim with weeping on my account while I was away in the army. She was so humble too, that when I opened a shop in our village with a partner, she would herself grind the medicines and spices which we sold with a pestle and mortar. I don't know why I felt so close to her, but I have noticed that many children do feel attached to one parent rather than to the other. Our Pritam for instance, if anything is wrong with her, no matter what, she will never open her heart to me, regardless of how much I press her to do so. She will only confide in her mother and only likes to sleep near her at night. Yet our little Pappi will never go with anyone else if I am present, not even his mother. He sleeps in my bed at night and sings his Daddy's praises all day long. Everyone in the house gives him affection – it is not that I make a greater fuss of him than the others. It must be the way he is made.

My father was not at all westernised. He was a very religious man and no doubt many would have called him old-fashioned. He had never had much education himself but he wanted us to study and sent us to school for as long as he could afford it. He was not a harsh father and hardly ever beat us, but he was very strict about attending school. One day my younger brother, Baldev, played truant, and when he found out our father was very angry. But all he said to my brother was, 'All right, just as you like. Don't go to school if you don't wish. But I shall expect you to help me with some work at home instead.' There was a pond near to our house and the next day Pitaji set Baldev to work fetching water and clay from the pond to make plaster for the house. He got so tired doing this all day that he was crying before the evening came. 'Right,' said our father. 'Now which do you prefer, going to school or staying at home and working?' Baldev didn't play truant again. But what does a child like that understand? He just likes playing and the whole world appears to him as one great game.

Chapter 4

GOING TO SCHOOL

UNTIL I was about twelve years old I used to attend a village school daily. We had to walk a few miles, for the nearest school was not in our own village but in another some way off. We used to set out early in the morning and come back at night. Sometimes we would play on the way back and it would be dark when we arrived home. But that was not often because we had to pass a little graveyard on the road home and we felt scared of going past it after nightfall.

I used to enjoy school very much, at least for the first few years. I can only tell you about boys' schools in India because there the boys and girls generally study in separate schools. In our village school there were five classes. There was a kind of introductory class for the beginners and four proper classes for the other pupils. There were two masters. One taught the upper three classes and the junior master taught the lower two classes. Lessons were usually held out of doors and all the little boys would sit on a cloth spread on the ground. The masters would sit on chairs and give them work to do. The senior master would appoint five monitors – one for each class – and give them each a badge to wear. Then they would help to supervise the others – children keeping children in order – so that the master need not get up from his chair.

We used to take our books to school tied up in a piece of cloth. We would squat on the ground with our books spread out around us and write with our slates resting on our knees. Sometimes we would go out into the jungle and cut bamboo branches and then make pens from the canes. Of course all our books and slates would often get mixed up and then there would be squabbles in the evening when it was time to clear up and go home. 'Who's got my slate? Give me my slate!'

Usually someone's books would get torn in the tussles that went on. All day we would be getting up to some sort of mischief – sometimes the little boys would get up and wander around or even piss on the ground when the master was not looking. It was not a big school you must remember, with a headmaster and nurse and a large staff like many schools over here. It was just a little village school. But we used to enjoy ourselves thoroughly. I can't tell you how much fun we had! But of course that was more than thirty years ago; I don't know what village schools are like nowadays. I can only speak from my own experience. We were carefree as small children and had no sense of time. All we knew was that when the bell rang in the morning it was time to run to school. There was a post-office in the same building as the school; in fact the junior master also acted as post-master and kept all the forms and papers used in the post-office in a big wooden box on his desk. When the mail arrived we knew that it was almost time for break. Then we would get out the food our mothers had prepared for us – *parathas* with mango pickle – and eat it out there in the open air. How different it was from an English school! There is no comparison at all.

The first time I went to school I did not enjoy it at all. My father took me along on my first day and when I saw the master scolding the boys I felt very scared. It seemed that my heart shrank with fear, and I remember how I cried. 'Things are not going to be easy here,' I thought to myself. Later I got used to being at school and was not afraid. Yet even so it is certainly true that in India the school-teacher is much more respected by his pupils than is the case in England. If the master told us, 'To-morrow the inspector is coming; let me see you all in clean new clothes,' then we would run home and cry until our parents promised that we should have new clothes. We were afraid that if we turned up without them the master would beat us. He would hit us with a great long cane – smack, smack, on the palms of our hands. My goodness, it was enough to put anyone into a state of alarm. We feared the master's anger more than that of our mothers and fathers, and would obey him no matter what happened. The village children respect no one so much as the school-master. One day, I remember, I fell ill and had to stay at home. I soon recovered but I was afraid to return to school in case the master should be angry at my absence. For two days more I lingered at home pretending that I was still too sick to attend, because I was afraid that he would beat me. In the end he came to our house himself and asked my father, 'What is the matter with your lad? He hasn't been coming to school for some days.' But when I heard my father propose that the master come and give me tuition at home as long as I was sick, I soon made up my mind that I would be well again the next day!

I stayed at that village school for about four years and then I graduated to a secondary school in the nearby town where I spent a further three years. So long as I was in the primary school I always stood first among all the pupils. I was a bright lad and liked studying. I learnt Hindi, English, even a little Sanskrit. But I was best of all at mathematics; I can remember my algebra even now. Yet in the sixth and seventh grades I did not do so well. I began to find the work very difficult. The school I attended was four miles from my home, and tramping that distance each morning and evening left me little time to do the homework in any case. And then much of the tuition at that stage was in English, which I found difficult. Again, there was no educated person at home or in the village to whom I could turn and ask, 'How should I tackle this translation? Please explain the meaning of this question.' If I had had some guidance at home I might have done well, but as things were I became a weak pupil. And the weak pupils got beaten for not doing well. So I began to lose my taste for studies. Then, once my father had lost all his money, I began to suffer on another account, for if a boy did not produce his fees he was made to stand on a bench all day as a punishment. The school fees used to be four rupees a month but my father had lost so much that he could no longer afford even this much. After I had completed the seventh standard he withdrew me from school and I was not sorry to leave. By then I had lost that former enjoyment and had become disgusted with the whole business of learning. 'What is the use of going to school now,' I thought, 'when I get nothing but beatings?' Later I realised that I had done the very thing I ought not to have done, as had I been educated I could have got a highly paid job. But if there is no bread in the house, how can a man send his sons to school? From that time on I had to struggle and suffer; I never again had the chance to sit and take life easily.

Chapter 5

FRIENDS AND PASTIMES

THE friends of my childhood were the sons of farmers, and often we would join in the work going on in the fields, for the villagers' life is the life of the land. Among my companions was Hemant; he was a Brahman by caste. Then there was Sadhu, a Jat, and Bhakhshi who was a Chamar. I have lost touch with them all now but I do know that Hemant later went to live in Delhi and had a job there as a painter and decorator. The rest must be working on the land still. There was a boy named Sital also, who came over here, or so I was told. I have never contacted him because I have no idea where he is staying. I only know that he is in England somewhere.

My other close companions were my younger brother – he is only three years my junior – and my elder brother's son. He was about seven years younger than myself and really lived in Delhi with his father. But he often came to stay in the village and when he was at our house he always joined my brother and me in our amusements. He did not live long, poor boy, for he died shortly after passing his tenth grade in school.

Our favourite pastime was playing cards – or if not cards, then marbles. If we could not get hold of real marbles we would use the fruit of a certain kind of tree. They are black and round, and we were just as happy to roll them about in the dust. In the right season we would go down to the well where there were cucumbers and melons growing and we would eat them sitting there in the shade. When the wheat harvest was gathered in we would run into the fields on a moonlight evening and play hide-and-seek in and out of the stacks of sheaves. Or else we would play *svaga*. You play *svaga* by forming two teams; the members of one team line up and form a kind of 'vaulting horse' by each bending over and clutching the waist of the boy in front. Then the members of the other team must run and vault on to their backs without falling or over-balancing.

How different it all was from England and from the amusements my children are used to over here! And yet who can say that we were not merry with these simple pastimes?

Chapter 6

LOW CASTE AND HIGH CASTE

THERE were families of many different castes living in our village. Mostly they were Jats, but there were also Brahmans, Julahas, Nais, Telis, Mirasis and Khatris. But as in most other Punjabi villages, the land-owning castes were in the majority. We learnt as children which castes were considered high and which low. Our parents would explain to us with which caste people we might eat and with whom it was forbidden. How else were we to learn if our mother and father did not teach us these things? Our family are Khatris, which are quite a high caste. They work mainly as shopkeepers and business men. A few of them own land but they are not really farmers by trade. We could therefore play with boys of lower caste, but we were not allowed to eat in their houses.

Of course whether you are respected or not as an individual depends on your character rather than on your caste, but if the majority of your caste fellows have bad habits they will give the whole caste an evil name whether you deserve it or not. There are low castes in our village who still eat filthy food, gipsy castes who feed on frogs and reptiles caught in dirty ponds. These low castes do not observe proper hygiene in their kitchens, or they eat half-finished food left over from other people's meals, a habit which we would consider unclean and disgusting. Some work in dirty occupations, such as sweepers and cleaners of latrines. Now who will want to eat with people who lead such a life, however worthy their characters? Ghandi tried to lift up the low castes but I do not think that his teachings were of much avail. Now the new laws allow the *Harijans* to enter the temples, but the older folk still would not enter them even if you were to drag them there forcibly. And the high castes are just as conservative. If throughout your life you have been taught to regard someone as filthy, a mere statute is not going to make you want to sit down and eat with him all of a sudden. After your death your son might be willing. But if you yourself have been accustomed to take a bath after even sitting near a member of those low castes you will not change so readily. If someone of my caste were to eat in a low-caste person's house by mistake, he would probably vomit straight away if he were to find out what their true caste was, such is the strength of one's upbringing.

Even in England, the low-caste people who come here still tend to treat members of the land-owning and farming castes rather respectfully, and the latter tend to look down on them in return. They continue to identify themselves with the caste or race they came from in India, regardless of the nature of the work they take up when they get here. But beyond this, people here do not bother with the details of caste rules as they do in India. After all, they mix with English people gladly enough, don't they? And even the English are dirty in their habits by strict high-caste standards. In one house where we used to live we shared a kitchen with a family of Chamars, a thing which would be quite unthinkable in India. But we do not worry over here, because no one is so fussy abroad.

Even when I went to live in Delhi I never used to bother much about caste, in fact in the town it is not always even possible to know for sure what caste a man really comes from. I only cared whether a man was a good man or a rascal; if a man is really good then his caste is of no consequence to me.

Chapter 7

A RELIGIOUS-MINDED MAN

My father was a religious-minded man, devoted to the practice of our Hindu rituals and worship, and his example had a deep effect on the development of my own temperament. While I was a child it is true that I took little heed of his precepts. What is this thing which people call God? I never gave the question a thought until the time when I left my parents' home and joined the army. But my father's teachings and practice must have worked on my mind slowly all that time, for now I take after him in my interests; I am truly his son in this respect.

For instance, he used to enjoy and seek out the society of men of religion, ascetics and *mahatmas*. He used to relate to me how when he was young he had observed a holy man practising penance by immersing his body in freezing water whilst performing his meditation. My father had a certain curiosity about these things and was of an experimental turn of mind, and so he considered whether he might not also try to do the same, and see how it was possible. He described to me how he had gone to the pond which is in our village one winter's day and sat down in the cold water there to perform his prayers. The moment he sat down in that pond, he told me, it seemed that the breath would altogether depart from his frame, such was the shock of the icy water on his body. But gradually the shock wore off, his body became accustomed to the chill and his mind so absorbed in his devotions that he no longer noticed the cold. Some of the feats which holy men perform, he would tell me, are done purely for show, to impress those who look on and are really only tricks. But in this case he found through his own experience that the power of prayer could really overcome bodily discomfort. I take after my father in this respect for I also enjoy the company of religious men and I always hope that I may learn something from them from hearing of their religious experiences. Now that I have come to England I should like to meet one of those Christian monks or nuns that lead an enclosed life and who have forsaken worldly things. I should like to talk to such a person and ask him many questions, but I do not know how I am ever to meet one.

In our village there was a temple at the crossroads where rituals were held every first Sunday of the month, and my father used to take me there very often when I was a little child. I would sit and listen to the hymns which they used to play there. One very famous musician from Pagvara used to perform at this temple quite frequently, and sometimes as many as a thousand people from the nearby villages would come to hear him. The high-caste people would sit in the main part of the room and the Chamars would sit to one side. All night long the musicians would sing hymns and narrate stories of the gods and sages, and the villagers would enjoy listening.

In Indian villages, all the family rituals like weddings, naming-ceremonies and funerals are performed by Brahmans, members of the highest caste. (Not all Brahmans are priests, of course; many have their own land and live as cultivators like the other villagers.) In our village, the Brahman priest would come round every month and inform us of the holy days which were to fall in that month, and remind us which fasts were to be kept and which rituals were to be observed. Of course most of the village Brahmans are not very learned but the villagers believe that they are the descendants of their *gurus* in olden times. In those days the Brahmans no doubt had inner wisdom which others did not possess. But such a quality cannot be perpetuated for ever down the generations; with time it is bound to be corrupted and the modern Brahmans are far from being as wise as their forebears. Yet people still respect them and think it meritorious to give them charity on feast days and special occasions. Some people in our village would make a point of feeding Brahmans regularly in the name of some *guru*. The Brahmans do not go begging for such gifts, far from it. People invite them of their own accord. When I went to live in Delhi I used to invite a Brahman to take a meal at our house once every month. I remember him well; he was a compounder in a dispensary and originally came from Multan. He would visit us regularly to receive our charity. Of course I know that it does not really matter to whom you give charity. If you wish to be generous it is of no consequence who is the recipient of your gift. Feed any man in the name of God, and provided what you give him is justly obtained and not at the cost of another man's blood then there is benefit in the action for you. But the Brahman is a convenient customary recipient of charity and even now that we have come to England we sometimes invite acquaintances of ours who are Brahmans to a meal at our house when we perform any religious ceremony.

It was through looking on at the religious rites and customs which my parents practised in our village that I received my religious education. I did not give a thought to spiritual matters at the time but when I grew up I came to appreciate what I had learnt from my father. I came to realise that only firm faith in God ensures a tranquil mind.

In the same way I try to teach my children now that I am also a father. When I worship, my children look on just as I used to look on in the temple. Look at this little baby of ours. I have already taught him to fold his hands as we do when we worship. When it occurs to me I remind him, '*Jay ker*'[1], and he does it. Of course, he does not know the meaning of the gesture at his age, but when he is older he will understand and these things will become a part of his very blood.

1. These words mean 'make a respectful greeting' or 'fold your hands'.

Chapter 8

KARMA

I WAS hardly ten years old when our family fortunes suffered a sharp turn. Until then, if we had not been wealthy then at least our life had been secure and comfortable; overnight we became poor. This is how it came about.

My father had given my elder brother an excellent education and had sent him to Lucknow University to take a course in engineering there. Those had been prosperous days for us and he could afford the expense. It was in 1929 that my brother qualified as an overseer – how many long years ago it seems now! Yet in spite of his qualifications he was unfortunate and was unable to find a job anywhere. Because of this he became discouraged and discarded the idea of becoming an engineer in favour of entering business like our father. He asked Pitaji to advance him his capital of Rs. 10,000 so that he could start trading as a corn dealer.

Now in the town of Pagvara there is a corn exchange, and Jagdish invested the whole sum of money our father had given him there. But in such places most of the business is conducted by word of mouth; one trader will tell another, 'I will take one hundred sacks of your wheat,' but few receipts are given or records kept of the deals which they make. And where the words on a man's tongue are the only evidence of a transaction there is much room for the inexperienced to stumble. Within a short time Jagdish had lost the whole of the money our father had given him, never to see it again. In those days Rs. 10,000 would buy much more than it would to-day, so the loss of so great a sum was a blow from which our family could never recover.

Apart from this misfortune, shortly after this my father had the further ill luck to break his leg, an injury which never properly mended, as that leg was to give him trouble for the rest of his life. The effect of these events on my father's mind was such as to discourage him absolutely from further efforts. He was an intelligent man, but all men fly where money is to be found, and though of a religious mind he was not other-worldly. His peace of mind was tied up with his money and he had not the indifference to mere material wealth which my mother showed. After losing all his money he was a disappointed man and had not the heart to apply himself to making a fresh beginning. If your plans are all dashed to the ground, everyone lets you down and you are disappointed in all your endeavours, what consolation is there when you are no longer a young man and are so unable to start up something new? And if a person's mind is so depressed by ill fortune that he feels that life has dealt him only injustice, then he has not the energy to succeed in any case. When a man loses faith in himself he is finished. He is the same man, his environment has not altered, but whereas before he was successful in whatever he put his hand to, now he fails. This was the state of mind in which my father remained after receiving these blows.

Even more troubles were to follow, for he was obliged to sell the land which he had owned in Bikaner. He had bought it at the time when his business was flourishing but now he had to dispose of it in order to make ends meet. And soon he was forced to withdraw Baldev and myself from the schools we had been attending. Neither of us was able to finish his schooling, for if a man has no money for food, how can he pay for education?

In the years that followed, death was to deal us many more sorrows. Jagdish eventually took a job in Delhi and sent his son to school there – the same boy who had been our playmate in the village. On the day that he heard that he had passed his examination in the tenth grade my brother sent him out to buy some melons by way of celebration. He set off on his bicycle but at the cross-roads in Pahar Ganj he met with an accident and fell from his cycle. He was taken to hospital immediately with a broken arm, but three days later he was dead.

In the hospital he had been overcome with a fever, the water went to his brain and he died. His mother, my sister-in-law, could not bear this loss; although she had another son and a little daughter besides, her grief was too much for her and within a couple of years she too died. Nor did my brother survive long. All these sorrows coming on top of the financial disaster he had suffered were too much for him to bear. His heart was broken and he could not live. He died only a year or two after my marriage.

When death dogs a family there is no escape. My elder sister had been married to a man living in District Jalandhar when I was only a small boy. His village was only about five miles from ours and I had a very good relationship with the members of his family. As a boy I used to visit my sister quite often and I always enjoyed staying at her house. But she was destined to spend only a couple of years in her married home, for she too died leaving only a little girl behind. That poor girl was to lead a miserable life and died herself at an early age.

Now that my parents are also dead there is no one of our near kin left in the village. My closest relative is my younger brother who now lives in Delhi. My father had no brothers or sisters, only two cousins on his father's side. Their sons still maintain a store in that same village where we used to live and one has lately come to England to live. In fact he lives not far from here and we visit him quite often. Apart from these we have no one left, and when we last came away from our village we locked the doors of the house behind us.

To this day I do not understand what my father did to deserve all these sorrows. Some people say that such troubles come as a result of evil spells. If a man injures another without justification then the ill-will which springs from the mind of his victim has the effect of a curse upon him. But what great injury my father could have done to another – so great that even his offspring was not protected from the evil which resulted – I could not tell.

Or perhaps it is a matter of *karma*, that in some previous life he committed some error. Many people here do not believe in karma but I am sure that if a person does wrong he eventually suffers misfortune as the consequence of his deeds, if not in this life then in some future birth. When the fruits of his wrong-doing fall on his head he bewails his lot and cries to the world, 'Alas, what shall I do, how have I deserved this?' for he does not remember his actions in his past lives. Perhaps this is why my father was so dogged by ill luck and sorrow, but I cannot say for there is no kind of learning which will reveal to us what we did or suffered in former births.

Chapter 9

EARNING A LIVING

In those days I saw what poverty was really like. After my father had withdrawn me from the school he sent me to work for a shop-keeper in another village. I was only a lad but my parents could not afford to keep me at home, now that our family fortunes had sunk so low. For several years I worked for that shop-keeper, living at his house and going home to my parents' village only occasionally on feast days and holidays. I used to receive my board and lodgings there, plus two rupees a month to take home with me. In the village it is not unusual for children to work for their living if their parents are poor. In any case the children of the craftsmen begin to learn their fathers' trades early in life. The carpenter's son is at work with his little hammer and plane when only a small boy. How other-wise will he learn the skills of his caste except by continual practice? Children who are obliged by poverty to work for others are in a very vulnerable position and I have often seen them exploited by unscrupulous men. If their parents are needy, as mine were, they are not in a position to grumble if their boy is overworked or not fed well. They have to be grate-ful that they are relieved of the burden of his keep. Yet I was quite lucky in this respect and although I worked in several different shops before joining the army, some of them miles from my father's village, I was fairly well treated on the whole – probably because I was efficient at the work I had to do. And in spite of the wretched pay, I enjoyed this work. I was happy doing it compared with the misery I had endured in the last two years at school. I learnt my duties quickly as I was quite intelligent, and I was relieved to be doing something I was good at again. I could remember exactly where everything was in the shop; if a customer came and said, 'I want some *sonf*,' I knew exactly where to lay my hands on the *sonf* without having to rummage around and keep the people waiting. I had such a good memory I could find everything in a trice.

Chapter 10

JOINING THE ARMY

As soon as I was eighteen I left this work in order to join the army. I had never intended to become a soldier and I was not really fitted for fighting by temperament, but I understood that the pay was good. Although by now my elder brother had found some work in Delhi, our household affairs were hardly thriving and it was essential that I should look for as well paid a job as I could find, now that I was older. One day I happened to meet a boy from our village who had joined the army some time previously and he began to paint a very attractive picture of the military life. If I joined up, he said, I should earn forty-eight rupees a month on recruitment and sixty after training, over and above my board and lodgings. Of course, to a boy who has been earning only two rupees a month this seemed an opportunity to be seized upon and I said, 'Take me with you and I will join up too.' To my father I said, 'Pitaji, let me go into the army and become a soldier.' My mother did not want me to go because it was war-time, but my parents consented in the end because they too thought that I should get good wages.

As it was war-time the officers were not too particular about whom they accepted for service. They could not pick and choose or stipulate that a recruit had to be so tall, educated to such-and-such a grade, or that his health must be up to a certain standard. So I was accepted even though I had not got a very strong constitution. Indeed, when I first joined up I was barely strong enough to lift my rifle and kitbag by myself.

It was only once I had joined up and signed all the papers that the real truth came out that I would only receive eighteen rupees a month for my services. That man had deceived me and I had been too trusting to disbelieve his word. Why had he lied? The fact was that he was really a recruiting agent and received a commission for every boy he duped into coming to the recruiting centre, no matter what means of persuasion he had used. As soon as I realised that I had been tricked I began to despair. I prayed daily to God, 'Bhagvan, how shall I manage on eighteen rupees a month? How can I send anything home to my mother and father?' So I entreated God to show me some way of securing my discharge.

It is my experience that there are no honest men in this world. If anyone has dealt me kindness, then at some time he has also dealt me pain. You may find a few who are prepared to give you good measure but they will always hope that there will be some benefit for them also in the action afterwards. No one will help you unless he sees some profit in it for himself. Have you ever seen a shop where the shopkeeper buys up his stock at two rupees per item and sells them at only one and a half rupees each? You will never find such a shop anywhere in the world, because the very purpose of shopkeeping is to make a profit – to give less and receive more. Everyone will try to make ten rupees on goods that are only worth two. That is how men treat people like myself who are trusting and naïve. There are some experiences I have had which are so painful to me that I do not know whether I suffer more by telling them or by hiding them in my heart. This first disillusionment of mine made me wonder whom I could trust in life and to whom I could ever turn for help.

Chapter 11

A NEW RECRUIT

It was in 1943 that I first joined the army. After I had signed up at Phillaur I was taken to Jalandhar to await training. At that time they were recruiting here, there and everywhere and all the new recruits were sent to the depot at Jalandhar. As soon as twenty or thirty new men had arrived there they would be formed up into a squad. Then each man would be equipped with his kit and the squad dispatched along with an officer to wherever their training was to be carried out. It was all done as quickly as possible because it was war-time.

No sooner had I been in the barracks in Jalandhar for a few days than I realised that the military life was not going to be easy. It was winter then and when they roused us early each morning it was cold enough to make a man weep. 'What have I committed myself to now?' I wondered. But it was too late to withdraw as I had already taken the oath. We were not allowed out of the barracks at all until we had been sent for training. About twenty of us were posted to Karia, near Jhelum (now in Pakistan) and there I was instructed as a driver for the Motor Ambulance section. We were taught how to drive the military trucks, how to mend them if they broke down, and all that it was necessary to know about their maintenance and how they worked. For thirteen weeks I spent the whole of each day learning about motors, nothing else. Because of the war they needed our services as soon as they were available. I did not dislike the work itself and I passed my tests easily in the thirteenth week. When I first saw a diagram pinned upon the wall, showing all the parts of the motor I was to drive, my heart sank. 'How shall I ever memorise all that?' I wondered. But then I remembered the shop where I had worked. Had I not come to know and remember where each item was kept, even though there were so many? And I began to feel some confidence again. I have a quick brain and do not find it difficult to pick up new skills.

But the life there was very rough. It was so fucking cold that when we were standing outside on guard it was not enough to wear just a greatcoat over your battle dress to keep warm. We used to take three blankets apiece and wrap them round our shoulders to keep out the cold. Even then I still used to feel chilly.

And then there used to be an inspector who would go with us in the trucks and ask questions about their maintenance to test our knowledge. If anyone made a mistake he used to give them a good slap. Another punishment he used to give was to make the offender run in front of the truck while he drove it along behind him. That was a rotten thing to do because the poor fellow would soon be exhausted yet the inspector would go on chasing him in the truck. There was one boy who was really terrified of that bully, as the inspector used to pick on him especially. He would sit at the steering wheel asking questions and if the poor boy got one wrong he would get so furious that he would leave go of the wheel to twist his ears with both hands. Not only was his victim nervous of being punished but the rest of us were nervous that the lorry would leave the road and crash when he did this! So I said to the boy, 'Don't go out with him alone. I will come with you and sit between you and then he won't be able to get at you.'

The boys there came from many different parts of India – some from U.P., some from C.P.[1] People sent from all directions ended up sitting in that centre. Many of them were just

1. 'U.P.' stands for 'Uttar Pradesh' a part of Northern India. 'C.P.' stands for 'Central Provinces', since Independence known as Madhya Pradesh.

naïve villagers and were confused by their new surroundings. Once I remember a chap who was not accustomed to using a latrine fell right into the sewage. You see, in the days of the British there were few flush lavatories in India. In the training centre we just used to dig a ditch and then cover it with wooden boards so as to make a kind of simple latrine. Well, that poor boy did not know how to use it properly – he over-balanced and fell right in, up to here. We had to fish him out and clean the filth off him. We couldn't help laughing at his predicament. I suppose we amused ourselves sometimes in spite of the hard life.

Chapter 12

ROUGH COMPANY

In the army I found myself in really rough company. You see, in war-time they could not be choosy about whom they accepted for service. Thieves, good-for-nothings – all the lay-abouts well known in their villages for their worthlessness – they would all get into the army. They were not a well-disciplined lot. Sometimes as many as twenty of them would be involved in a brawl together.

All day and all night we had to take it in turns to stand on sentry duty, each doing a stint of two hours at a time. If one of these rough characters was on duty he would be sure to come and wake you up at least half an hour before your turn was really due. 'Get up, mate, it is your turn,' he would say. By that time you would be really wide awake so there was not much you could do about it. But when you came off duty and had to wake him up, he would say, 'All right, I am just coming,' and then go right back to sleep again. You could not make him wake up if he didn't want to take his turn. They were real bastards, the whole lot of them.

And then they had another fiddle. All our clothes and kit were marked with our numbers so that they could be identified. Every so often there would be a kit check to see that we all had the kit we were issued with, pants, sweaters, towels, boots and so forth. These fellows would form gangs with their pals, usually the men who came from the same village as themselves. Then they would pinch your towel or shirt or socks and hand them to some member of their gang who was in a different platoon. So when it was your platoon's turn to have a kit check, that item was nowhere to be found, of course, however hard you searched. These rascals would be able to produce all their gear with the right numbers marked on them, but if you were caught with your socks or boots missing then you were really in trouble. Then when one of them got leave to go home on a visit he would collect up all the stuff the members of his gang had hidden, take it back to the village and distribute it among his family and his friends' families.

I remember that one of the first things the officer taught us when we were in training was, 'When you go to the front, fire on any enemy soldier you sight, without asking questions. If you don't, he will get you first. Never mind whether he is a rogue who deserves death or an honest fellow like the rest; so far as you are concerned he is just an enemy.' And this I have found to be true of all situations in life. If you don't stand up for yourself everyone will take advantage of you. The word gets round that 'This chap never hits back' and everyone comes and preys upon his peaceable nature. But if, once someone harms him, he gives them a good slap in return and tells them to be gone, then he will be respected and no one will trifle with him again. I know that it would have been better for me if I had had that kind of strength to make sure no one troubled me, but being a peaceable man I was often the victim of such tricks in the army. I am still like that, though I know well that it would be better for me if I were more aggressive. It is not in my nature to hit back though I often wish that I were otherwise.

In the army they were very strict with the men. When I was

in the training centre there were plenty of others like myself who realised that they had made a blunder in joining up, or who tired of the hard conditions there. Deserters would run away if they got the slightest opportunity, but usually in the end they were caught and hauled back, their hands tied with ropes. In the evening there would be a roll call, at about nine or ten at night, and the deserters would be brought before the whole company. The officers would black their faces in front of all the men in order to shame them, and then jeer at them. The *havildar* or quartermaster would taunt them, 'Oh, so his lordship has turned up again, has he?' Sometimes the officers would even spit in a deserter's face. I have seen all this with my own eyes; it is the truth I am telling you. It was all supposed to be an example to the rest of us.

They had more complicated punishments too. Sometimes we had a kit parade, which everyone hated as it meant trooping about in the hot sunshine with all your kit strapped on your back and your rifle in your hand. The officers would be standing in the shade of the trees and the inspector would shout the orders from there, 'Right turn, forward march, about turn.' Some people would try to avoid all this by pretending to be ill and getting sick leave. But if the officers suspected that those who were supposed to be sick were not really ill they would order them to report to the *subedar* or whoever was on duty early in the morning. They would have to carry over all their kit – which weighed all of twenty *sers* – and lay it out on the floor for inspection; blankets, overcoat, boots, the lot. Then they would have to pack it all up again and take it back to their quarters. They would make the lead-swingers do that three times a day, just to harass them. In the army a man is really disciplined, he is really straightened out.

Chapter 13

1947

AT the time of the riots in 1947 I was still in the army.[1] I worked with the driver of a lorry as his cleaner. That meant that I accompanied him on long journeys, attended to the maintenance of the motor, and carried out any repairs which might be necessary. Travelling up and down the Punjab I saw more suffering at that time than I care to recall. At the time of Partition the government set up camps for the refugees and whenever we had to visit one of these camps in the course of our work my heart used to ache with pity for those people – some poor, some ill, all helpless. In one camp I saw several hundred graves where those who had been killed in the riots were buried. People did such evil to each other; in the fighting some were stabbed, some beaten, even children and old men and women were murdered. I have seen an innocent baby picked up and speared with its mother looking on. Hindus killed Muslims and Muslims slaughtered Hindus. No one asked whether the other deserved it. And besides the killing there was looting and thieving. Hindus were guilty as well as Muslims. One could not say that one side offended more than the other. In time of civil war men's violence is unbridled. They throw off all controls and abuse anyone they like because the

1. In this chapter Rampal is referring to the civil unrest which preceded the granting of independence to India in 1947. Communal rioting and killing took place between Muslims on the one hand, and the Hindus and Sikhs on the other, and the Punjab (where large numbers of each of these groups lived in close proximity) was one of the worst affected areas. In 1947 the subcontinent was partitioned into the new states of Pakistan and India. Many of the Muslims in India fled to Pakistan, and almost all the Hindus and Sikhs in Pakistan fled to India. The old Punjab Province was split into two parts by the new border between Pakistan and India.

whole of society has gone mad. No one asks another, 'Why have you committed this cruelty?'

In our village there was much fighting. One day especially stands out in my mind, there was such bloodshed. I saw with my own eyes a little boy – he could not have been more than nine or ten years old – entreating with folded hands the man who was butchering his father, 'Don't kill him, don't kill him.' The murderer took no pity but after killing the father turned on the child and cut off his hands. This happened before my very eyes, and it grieves me to recall the scene. There were even worse things than that, but I could do nothing because I was afraid myself. I am not so bold that I dare step in and stop people when they are in a mood to commit atrocities like that.

The day after that riot the villagers brought bullock carts and loaded them high with corpses, just as they load the sugar at harvest time. Then they took them all to a mass grave and buried them there.

Of several thousand inhabitants of our village about one thousand were Muslims. When they heard that India was to be partitioned the others told the Muslims, 'If you want to stay here you must give up Islam!' They had to agree; what else could they do? So they were taken to the *gurudvara*. Each was given a *kara* and by taking *prasad* was made a Sikh. The others told them, 'Now brothers, you must give up smoking both cigarettes and *hukka*. Tobacco is forbidden to you now that we have made you Sikhs.' And what sort of Sikhs were they? They had failed their own faith but they had abandoned it under pressure. For fear of death they ate what Islam forbade them to eat, but their hearts were not changed. Nor were they ever really accepted by the Sikhs, for when violence broke out again their conversion seemed to have made no difference. So when the army moved in and offered to give those who wished to go to Pakistan safe conduct, all those Muslims went off. 'We are not staying here,' they said – and indeed if they had they would certainly have been killed. Not a single Muslim is left in our village now.

I do not know why people try to convert others to their own

religion. Of course, if you ask me I will say that I am a Hindu. For me Hinduism is the best of religions. How should I say otherwise? Everyone prefers his own faith, naturally. But I cannot say that Hinduism is the only good religion or that it is right for everyone. In any case religion is only a matter of opinion. If a Hindu becomes a Muslim he changes only his ideas, not his nature. He is still a human being and his basic needs are the same. All men are born with the same purpose in life – to serve God – and whether they sing his praises after the Muslim fashion, in the Christian way or according to Hindu precepts does not matter. But every man whatever his religion needs clothes, needs warmth, feels hunger and thirst. Can I say to a Muslim, 'Become a Hindu and you will no longer feel hunger?' Of course I cannot. Therefore why do people try to convert others?

Wherever you look there is fighting going on somewhere in the world. In 1947 Hindus and Muslims were fighting each other in India, now Americans and Communists are fighting each other in Vietnam. War never ceases. Often it is the people who are closest to each other who fight the most bitterly. Hindus and Muslims lived side by side in India for so long. They lived in the same villages and worked the same land. Yet they fought so fiercely. I suppose it is no different from family quarrels. The members of one household are joined to each other and yet they still fight amongst themselves. Mother wars with daughter, father disputes with son, brother quarrels with brother. One son is jealous of the love his parents give to his brother, one sister feels that the other does not love her and complains that she is never invited to the other's house. It seems that the enmity of those who are closest to each other is also the most bitter. That is how it was in the civil war of 1947 – so bitter that I hope never to see such scenes again.

Chapter 14

THE OFFICERS' CHILDREN

It was while I was still in the army that the desire to go to England first entered my heart. Most of our officers were Indian – the *havildar*, the *naik*, the quartermaster and the *jemadar* were all Indians – but our captain was an Englishman. He was a good man and I looked up to him for he used to treat us well. In the barracks we used to see other English officers and their families. I would watch their little fair children and wonder at them. They looked so beautiful, it seemed that even the dust was not allowed to settle on their clothes. Sometimes you see a thing so beautiful to look at, that more than look you dare not. You fear to stretch out a hand to touch it. That is how I felt watching those little English children, so I just looked at them, only looked. Perhaps I might have spoken to the English people but I did not know their tongue.

But what impressed me most was the fact that all the English people we saw were rich. Naturally people are impressed by the way a man looks. Among our Indian folk also, when a rich man passes by, the people who see him think in their hearts, 'Yes, here is a *raja*, here is a man of wealth, a man blessed by fortune.' His appearance proclaims his riches. In the same way when we looked at the English people, there was not one poor man amongst them. What sort of country must theirs be?

As well as this I had seen how Indians who had gone to work overseas lived. They were able to send so much money from abroad, and when they returned they bought acres of land and built palatial houses for themselves. Seeing these people sowed curiosity in my heart that I also might go to *vilayat* and see that wonderful place. Around me were men with little to eat, little to drink, and I myself had little money. What could eighteen rupees a month buy? Yet what sort of place could this England be that everyone who went there came back a rich man and lived in such luxurious ease? I began to realise that there might be places in the world free of the drudgery and poverty which I saw around me; I had something to compare my own environment with and I saw that there must be a world of difference between India and England. Surely the difference must strike you also, if you make an honest comparison?

Therefore I began to pray in my heart, 'Oh *Bhagvan*, if only you would send me to England also, then I might see for myself the life they lead there.' If someone had told me at that time, 'Rampal, some day you will indeed go to England and you will suffer much unhappiness there,' I would not have believed it, but at least what I saw first awoke in me the wish to see England for myself. That desire was never to leave me in the years to follow, until at last I arrived here.

Chapter 15

LEAVING THE ARMY

I BECAME more and more miserable in the army. The pay was low and I was not suited to the rough life and rough company there. As soon as I began to compare myself with others I wondered why I had allowed myself to be trapped in this way. 'Now I am stuck here,' I thought, 'If only I could escape somehow.' For I remembered my mother, my father, and Baldev; I wanted to provide for them now that they needed my help, but what could I do on such little pay? I could see no way out of my difficulty; having entered the contract I could not leave the army at will, for the matter of my discharge was outside my control.

Before that time I had never prayed regularly but now I began to entreat God daily to help me in my trouble. In the barracks there was a mosque for the Muslims, a *gurudvara* for the Sikhs and a temple for the Hindus. One day I went to the temple thinking that I would ask the *pandit* there for advice as to how I might secure my discharge. He told me that if I were to recite a special prayer to Hanuman[1] every day for some time then surely Hanuman would grant my wish. So each morning I used to rise early and go to the Hanuman temple and recite this prayer there. I memorised the whole of it during that time.

From the very moment that I began to worship daily my life started to change. First of all I was posted to Hyderabad. It was my duty to drive trucks between Poona and Hyderabad (for I was an experienced driver by then). Once there, I began to develop eye trouble. My eyes hurt and my eyesight became poor. So from Hyderabad I was sent to Lucknow, where the record centre of the army was, to find out whether the trouble was serious enough to warrant my discharge. While I was in Lucknow I continued to pray daily in the temple there. At first I used to go there wearing my army boots, which I would leave outside the temple door. But one day they were stolen from where I had left them while I was inside performing my devotions. I took that as a sign that in future I should not even wear shoes on the way to the temple and after that I would walk there barefoot.

I visited the army doctor in Lucknow several times and he asked me how my eyes had first started to give me trouble. I replied that they had only begun to hurt since I had been working in the army. Before that they had been perfectly all right. When he examined me he said, 'Yes, this man's eyesight is certainly weak. In my opinion he should be discharged.' He filled in the necessary forms and papers and sent them to the members of the board who were to examine my case. The board consisted of five or six men. The day before my case was to come before them I went to the temple as usual and prayed that they would agree to my discharge. As I sat in the temple I had, as it seemed, a vision of Krishan *Bhagvan*;[2] he appeared clearly

1. Hanuman is a Hindu deity.
2. Krishna, or Krishan, is the incarnation of the Hindu deity Vishnu.

and distinctly before my eyes. The very next day I learnt that I was indeed to be discharged and sent home. This is the complete truth that I am telling you.

If a man puts all his faith in God, then God will surely fulfil all his desires. No matter what is his need – whether he desires wealth, whether he desires a son – if his mind is fixed on God and he sees only God before his eyes, then automatically his wishes are granted. Sometimes I think more about the hundred pounds' worth of premium bonds I have bought, and sometimes I think less, but if I were to keep my mind on them one hundred per cent of the time then I would certainly win. It is the same with God. When I prayed to God to release me from the army which I hated, my mind became concentrated upon Him; it became fastened upon this prayer and so God granted his help.

It was this incident which started me on the path of devotion. When a man is eaten up with despair of the world he may seek solace in various ways. If he is much attached to the things of the material world already then he may commit suicide. He does this because material things have already made him that he can see nothing beyond them. But if it is not too late then he may turn to God in his misery. Finding no peace elsewhere he begins to pray. And God, like a father who is so touched by his son's affection to give the boy greater and even greater love, comes to know that someone is remembering Him. When you remember God, He comes and sits in your heart and then improvement in your fortune is sure. This is how my longing to leave the army and to return home came to be fulfilled.

Chapter 16

RAMPAL'S SHOP

WHEN at last I came home from the army I began to think how best I might now earn my living. A friend of mine suggested that we open a shop together and I liked the idea. I approached my father and asked him if he could provide me with a little capital to start the venture off with. You do not need much money to establish a little store in a village like ours. The people are not rich and they only spend a little money at a time – a packet of spices, a reel of thread, a pair of bootlaces, a few ounces of salt. They make little purchases like these and so you can make a small beginning with only a few hundred rupees' worth of goods and build up your business from there. But my father had been so disappointed in my elder brother's failure that he had no inclination to part with the little money he had at the time nor take another risk with it. He threw in twenty or thirty rupees and the rest I had to provide myself, although he and my mother – even my mother – used to work in the shop alongside of me, preparing medicines and powders. How hard my mother worked I cannot describe to you. What a good woman she was!

I did not bear my father any grudge for his refusal to give me more help, for I understood the reasons for it. He was a sad and broken man so I did not resent him for not helping me.

We sold all kinds of goods in our shop – chutney, spices, pickles, scent, *pan*, cigarettes, even charcoal for the villagers' braziers. I had worked in a shop before of course, and so I knew how everything should be kept. And I even knew all the properties of the various medicines we sold. My associate was a *hakim* and we specialised in selling medicines and drugs. In India some people take drugs like opium and hemp and my

58

friend the *hakim* used to order these for some of our customers who were addicts. I noticed how their addiction used to affect these men morally. They would become jealous of each other and if the *hakim* served one while the other was looking on, then the latter would watch carefully to see that the other was not getting something superior to what he had received himself. Sometimes one would say, 'Hakim *Sahib*,' (that is what they used to call my friend) 'why do you give all the good pieces to the others and not to me? I can't get a fix from this stuff.' His heart would burn with jealousy. Or when a man came to buy hemp he would say, 'First show me your hemp.' We used to sell it in blocks, so I would show him one and he would say, 'Cut it from that side – no, the other side is better.' Well, it was the same all the way through, of course, there was no difference between one side and the other, but so strong was the dependence of these men on their drugs that they became weak and petty characters through their addiction. It depressed me to see these men squabble among themselves over such trivial things.

However it was not because of this that I eventually decided to abandon shop-keeping. The trade in the village was not sufficient to win us the income we had hoped for, the business did not really flourish. The most you could say was that we just about managed to earn our bread. I kept on for a full year but in the end decided that I stood a better chance of getting a secure income if I went to seek work in the city. And so in 1948 I left my village for good and went to join my elder brother in Delhi.

Chapter 17

DELHI

I WAS lucky enough to find work in Delhi almost immediately. I got a job in the Central Public Works department as an apprentice electrician. First of all I was sent to work in a wireless station. Thirty rupees a month was what they gave the apprentices – not a great deal better than the eighteen rupees I had been receiving in the army, and even then I had to buy my own food and clothing, which had been provided free in the army. But being government service the job was secure and the wages were gradually increased both according to my experience and in accordance with the rising cost of living. They would go up by five rupees one year, ten the next. Later when I had qualified as a wireman I started to receive Rs. 175 a month. At first I stayed with my elder brother and his family. But I did not get on well with his wife and after only a short time I left and started to live on my own, so as to avoid getting involved in family quarrels. She died a couple of years after I left and then I returned to Jagdish's house to live there for another year until his death. When I arrived in Delhi the city life was not so novel and unfamiliar as it might have been for many a villager coming to work in the big city for the first time. Remember that I had been in the army, and in military service a man gets to know about life. I had travelled all over India, seen jungles, rivers, cities, mountains. There was little in India that could be strange for me. In any case I had visited towns when I was a little child with my father. I remember how as a small boy I had stared in amazement to see so many tall buildings. 'What sort of houses are these?' I used to say to myself in wonderment. I would hang about outside the railway station, gazing at the trains coming and going. Everything that

I saw in the town astonished me at that time. But on coming to the city as an adult these things no longer seemed strange and unfamiliar.

Even so, after the slow life of the village I still found myself surprised by the hustle and bustle of Delhi. How odd the people looked, rushing here and there, and everywhere it seemed there were crowds of men and women. On every roadside there were stalls – on some roasted corn cobs were being sold, on others *bidis* or orange squash. And how the water gushed from the taps – quite different from the wells in our village!

As I moved about the city I could not help becoming more and more aware of the squalor and poverty in some of the quarters. I myself was well provided for, as I had found work quickly, but the unhappiness of others still pained me. There are slums on the other side of the Jumna where the poor people have put up little huts for themselves; no one asks why the people living in those shacks are fated to be so poor. No one cares whether they live or die. And there are places where people throw ordure and dirt – such filthy places that you would not be able to bear to stand there. In fact I will give you a hundred rupees if you are prepared to sit down there for one minute. If you see such places you will pray to God that you never have to live in such squalor yourself. I too began to pray before God, '*Paramatma*, take me to some country where I shall not have to see such terrible things, or else let me die.'

Chapter 18

GETTING MARRIED

A FEW years after I left the army, when I had been working in Delhi for some time earning my own keep, I got myself married. I say got 'myself' married, but what was there for me to arrange? My parents did it all for me. They felt that our household circumstances were such that we could now afford to get me married and indeed that the whole thing should take place as soon as possible. They did not consult me – in India no one asks a boy or girl whether they want to marry or not. It is for their parents to decide, according to their convenience and finances. No one said to me, 'How would you like to get married now?' But I would not have refused even if they had. Why should I have? I wanted to be wed. My father was in the village still and he considered several girls before finally choosing Satya. This took some time, of course, for in our country it is the custom that the boy's parents do not take the initiative themselves. It is the girl's parents who spread the word around that their daughter is grown-up and needs a husband. It is they who wander from place to place in search of a suitable boy. The girl does none of the looking herself, for she is in the first flush of youth and cannot judge impartially. She is too liable to be moved by her passions. If a woman needs a man badly she is in no way to judge which man is best. Likewise if a man needs a woman he is the least qualified to make a good choice. Need blinds them to what is right. It is better that some loving person who desires their well-being should make the choice for them.

My parents-in-law came to know that my father was interested in getting me married and approached him about the matter. He had been asking people if they knew of a suitable boy for his daughter and someone told him that Rampal was now of a marriageable age and might make a good husband for

Satya. He came to meet me at my father's home to see what I was like. He must have taken a fancy to me for not long afterwards he told my father that he would like me for his son-in-law. In fact he liked my younger brother also for he said, 'We would like both your sons for our daughters.' So I was engaged to Satya and my brother to her younger sister. For three whole years we were engaged. I was strictly forbidden to visit my bride's house, or even her village. If by some chance I had been found in that village the relationship would have been broken off. That is the custom. My mother would have been allowed to see my bride, my sister could see her, but I myself was forbidden. Even after the wedding I hardly ever used to see my in-laws. Their village was about thirteen miles from ours and we were not on close visiting terms. I did not have much to do with them; after all, I needed nothing from them, nor they from me.

As soon as all the arrangements were completed, and as soon as we had enough money, it was time to consider a date for the wedding, so my father asked an astrologer to suggest an auspicious day. He consulted his almanac and told my father which day would be best – at what time the *lagan* ceremony should be held, and when the wedding rites should take place. So I received a letter from Pitaji saying, 'The date for your wedding is near. Be sure to get leave from your work in good time to come here.' And a month beforehand the women started dancing and singing in our house each day.

I paid for all the wedding festivities held at our house myself. Everything I had ever received I have worked for myself. To live in luxury is to eat what someone else has earned. Then you do not fret about the cost but enjoy yourself at ease. But my parents were never in a position to give me presents – a cycle or a car. All I had to be thankful for was that my parents were both alive and my two brothers had secure jobs.

Baldev and I were married together; it was a double wedding. There were some twenty or thirty men in our party at least, and we all stayed at my father-in-law's village for three days. We had a really good time, for they entertained us well.

After the wedding I went back to Delhi and Baldev returned to Bikaner where he was working at the time. Satya stayed on at her parents' house for a while and joined me in Delhi a little later.

In those days it was the custom for the bride to remain veiled all the time during the wedding. Some people have stopped this now, but until recently it was always like that. So my wife and her sister kept their faces hidden during all the ceremonies. We could not see what they looked like at all. Even after our marriage my wife always used to keep her face veiled before my father. I do not know how this custom began, but I think it is sensible in many ways. It is good to show respect and honour to one's elders and besides, if wife and father-in-law do not have too much to do with each other then they can't quarrel, can they?

One thing is quite certain in my mind, that it is best of all for people to marry without meeting each other beforehand. In India girls and boys do not mix before marriage so when bride and groom come together they have faith in each other's virtue and steadfastness.

I have never had any doubt whether my wife would stay with me or not. I have always had confidence in her because she never knew any other man but me, nor did I know any other woman. If a husband and wife have never met before, when they meet for the first time on their wedding night they find such love for each other as will never fail throughout their whole lives. All the arrangements for the wedding are their parents' work, but the love that they engender when they lie together on that first night is of their own making. That is how I felt when I first saw my wife on our wedding night. Just as something which is held in front of a camera is imprinted forever on the film in the space of one second, so my wife's face was imprinted in my heart on that first night. I began at that moment to feel that this woman was mine and I was hers.

My wife's temperament is quite different from mine. If she thinks of a thing, she wants to get up and do it at once. I need more time to reflect upon things. I brood over everything and worry much more than she does. But though we are so different, we get on very well together and seldom quarrel. For I have always thought it important to be honest with my wife about everything and always confide in her. Ours is an open and straightforward relationship. Of course we accept that we are bound to argue a bit at times, but we know that these little differences will pass. When Satya sees me annoyed she keeps quiet, and when she gets angry I keep quiet; you cannot help getting annoyed with each other sometimes. We are only scrupulous in that we never vent our annoyance before the children.

Now that we live in England we always have to remember that we are in a foreign country. If I alienate my wife or leave her, where shall I turn? Or if she is irritated with me, where can she go? If we were in India she could always take the children to her parents' house for a little rest. But we have no family here and if we start arguing or split up, what would become of our children? If one of us is really heated the other only has to say, 'All right, wait until we get back to India; we will see what people say over there!' Then we soon make up our difference.

Chapter 19

A TRUE FRIEND

I HAVE been a lonely man all my life. In this country I have made few friends, at least no close friends. Yet in Delhi I made one friend whose affection for me was deep and sincere. His name was Bishan Das. He worked in the same plant as myself, at least he did at first; later he was transferred to another division. You see, in the Public Works Department there are several different divisions – air-conditioning, desert cooler, electrical section, etc. We used to repair the machines used in the government offices to send hot air in winter and cool air in summer. Bishan Das and I became friends when we worked side by side but even after he was transferred we used to come and go, visiting each other regularly. There were ten or twelve of us working in the Public Works Department who were friendly with each other and every month or so one of us would invite the others to his home. He would provide food for the rest and we would hold a little party at his house. One of these friends of mine was an armature winder, another a carpenter; we all came to know each other through working in the same place.

Yet I had no friend so close to me as Bishan Das. Like me, he was not a native of Delhi but had come there from a little village in the foothills of the Himalayas. He was an intelligent and loyal man, and such was our friendship for each other that if one of us had hurt himself I think the other would have felt the pain. He was generous and affectionate to me as no other. When my sister's daughter was in hospital she was so ill that the doctors said that she would need to have a blood transfusion and they asked me to find someone willing to donate blood so that her life might be saved. I could not give blood myself because my constitution was weak, and so I approached many men whom I knew. But not one was prepared to give his blood. I did not know what I could do to save my poor niece but then Bishan Das said to me, 'Here, Rampal, I will give blood – as much as you need.' So we went to the hospital and they laid him on the table to draw his blood. 'Take as much as is necessary to save the girl,' he said. Look how much regard he must have had for me in his heart to do a thing like that! After all, it is no little thing to give your own blood.

One day Bishan Das approached me and said, 'Rampal, my wife and baby are in my village and I want to bring them to live with me in Delhi. But the room I am living in is very tiny and stuffy. In Delhi the heat is so great in summer and I do not want them to suffer.' I saw that here was an opportunity given to me to show my affection for him and return his kindness so I said, 'Why do you not come to share our room?' The room we were living in at that time was very spacious – at least eighteen by twenty-four feet – like a long hall – and would just about accommodate us all. So I urged him, 'Brother, come and live with us.' He brought his wife and baby daughter to Delhi and they stayed with us for some time. We all got along very well together for his wife – her name was Talavati – became friendly with my wife. They were so considerate that if ever they came in from outside they would always knock on the door first before entering. Now tell me – in one room we were all living and sleeping alongside each other, two couples and their children, and we were all happy together. Surely only a friendship which is deep and sure can make such a thing possible? It is hard for people to live on such terms with others unless there is very true affection between them. If you share a place with another you become acutely aware of all his ways, and critical of them. Or else he may dislike your habits and criticise them. You will tell him not to talk rubbish and then he will be angry with you. You are always in fear of killing the affection you have for one another. Even with my younger brother I did not have such harmonious relations as I did with Bishan Das. Even my own brother, when he was living with us, would sometimes pick on some little thing and argue about it, or I would get annoyed with him. It is usually like that when people live together (and I should know, since for most of the time I spent in Delhi I was sharing accommodation with someone else, first my elder brother, then Bishan Das, then my younger brother). Even between father and son, mother and daughter, trivial matters become causes of contention and disharmony. But if you live with someone you don't own them, so you cannot force them to conform to your own habits.

I do not write to Bishan Das or my other companions in Delhi. I don't even know where Bishan Das lives these days. I do not write to him because if I were to send him a letter he would feel obliged to reply and it would cost him nearly a rupee to send an air-letter. And a rupee is worth a great deal to poor people in India. Our friendship was so fine that I should not wish to spoil its memory by resentment over money –

money is the thing which spoils relationships sooner than any-thing else – nor do I wish to give him trouble. So I leave it at that and do not write. Besides, I know that if anything im-portant happens – if any of my friends is in trouble, if a son is born to one of them, or if any of them is ill, the news will reach me through my brother. When I send a letter to Baldev I always write, 'How is Bishan Das? Have you met him lately or not?' When we next go to India we shall see him again and hear all his news first hand.

Chapter 20

A VOUCHER FOR ENGLAND

THE longer I stayed in Delhi, the more convinced I became that the best thing for me would be to leave India and seek work in England, and the more I saw of the prosperity of those who had returned from *vilayat* with money and fine clothes, the more firm my conviction grew. But I did not know how I should go about it and indeed had little faith that it would be possible. For I could not see how I would be able to go when my family were not rich enough to finance me, neither were my wages high. Yet for at least fifteen years while I was living in Delhi I used to visit the *gurudvara* every week and bow down there. In my heart I would pray, 'Oh, God, other men go to England, yet I never had the chance. If only I could get work there myself.' Sometimes I would visit one temple, sometimes another, but my prayer was always the same. 'But,' I thought, 'it is a matter of fate whether I go or not; I can do nothing if God has not destined me to go.' Then when someone men-tioned to me that those who had served in the army under the British were given priority when it came to applying for vouchers, I determined that I really would go, and I began to save as much money as I could from my monthly wage with that end in view. I could see that for everyone in India life was a struggle to earn his daily bread. The farmer has to kill himself with work in order to produce enough grain every six months to make a thousand rupees – yet how long will that last him? Those who are employed by others sweat in order to earn a hundred rupees or two hundred – seldom more. And with that wage they have to keep their families for the whole month. Those who have their own businesses are rich enough, but how many are so fortunate? Even they are always in fear that their business may fail, that there may be no demand for their goods. Anyway, even if ten men in one hundred are rich it is insignificant; it means nothing to the others who are poor. As for the poor low caste people, Chamars, Chuhras, Bansis, those who live in huts and own nothing more than a couple of saucepans and a dog – a hundred rupees have never shown their face in their houses. They have to sing for their supper.

On the other hand, as I saw for myself, those people who had been to England came back wearing brand new suits and loaded with money. And all those who had daughters to marry would rush to their doors, be they old, ugly, stunted or lame. A man who brought two thousand rupees home with him could not fail to get a pretty wife; a man of seventy years would get a girl of twenty if he were rich. (What that poor girl would say to a father who had married her off in that way I do not know, but that is how it was.) And those who had been to *vilayat* to work could send money home each month and still afford to buy land or build a fine house in India on their return. Surely if they could do all this I could do the same? My living would be secure and my children would have a good education to start them off in life. Of course there would always be a few good-for-nothings who would not send a penny home but just enjoy themselves eating and drinking in England. But even they would be held in great awe when they came back to India just because they had been abroad. Many would lie about the marvellous things they had done in England and what great fellows they had been there, but how was a man like me to know what was the truth? I had no way of judging.

I would meet many people who had been to England and they would encourage me to apply for a voucher myself. There was a cousin of Satya's for instance, and an acquaintance of mine who worked in the Ministry of Education. So at last I applied for a voucher, filled in the forms and sent them off. I had no difficulty for soon I received a reply to say that my application had been successful and that I could go to England any time I liked. I was delighted that my prayers seemed to have been answered at last and was very optimistic about my future in England. I understood that the voucher I had received meant that I had been given a job as well as permission to enter England; I did not realise that it was only a permit to work there and that I should have to seek for a post on my arrival. So I thought to myself, 'Now that I have work over there I shall have no problems; no doubt it is only a labourers' job as I am not highly educated but I will work with a will, do as much overtime as I can, and in a month or two my wife and children will be able to join me.' I was quite sure that I would be able to earn enough for their fares in a very short time, certainly not longer than the money I was leaving with them would last them, and so the question of sending them money from England would not arise, or so I thought. Once in London there would be sure to be some Punjabi-speaking person who would willingly show me around. He would show me what to do and I would do as he said. God would make everything right for me. The only slight doubt I had in my mind that was my poor English would lead to difficulties. If an Englishman were to ask, 'What is your name?' would I be able to understand and answer in correct English? If I had to attend an interview my lack of English would make me helpless. But I did not worry much as I had it in my mind that many Indians had already gone to England and one of them would surely be prepared to take me under his wing until I was settled.

One man told me that in England, if you are out of work, the government gives you food and board until they can find you a job. If you are sick or old then also the government sees that you are fed. But no one told me that I should have to do every-thing for myself, find a job, search for accommodation, without any assistance or encouragement of any kind from others. And that even then I should not earn enough to bring my family over to join me at once but would have to wait a full year until I saw them again. At the time of my departure I had no premonitions of all that was to befall me and was sure that I would be happy and prosperous in England; at the very most I regarded it as a risk well worth taking.

I cannot understand now why other people misled me so and gave me such false impressions about England. Perhaps it was their cunning – that those who had visited England did not wish to admit that they had found life there hard themselves, and so they deliberately made it out to be far better than it really was. Those people who bear tales of the riches to be won in London are like the clerks which lawyers employ. The clerk's business is to bring clients to the lawyer who is his master; the lawyer does not have to do anything himself. The clerk does the talking and acts as go-between, even if he gives a completely false idea of what the lawyer can really do. He can create misunderstandings if he chooses to so do, just as those who encouraged me to come here did.

But it is very likely that many of the people who told me so much about the marvels of life in England had never been there themselves and really knew nothing about it. Living in a place alongside its people, and merely hearing about it from other people are two different things. Over there, what conception could we form about England without seeing it for ourselves? It would have been just as difficult for us to form a true picture of England as it would be for an English person over here to form a true picture of India merely from hearsay and what he read in the papers.

The very distance between England and India makes it difficult for people in the one to grasp any clear idea of conditions in the other. It is so far away that it seems unreal. And I have to admit that even if I had been given a truthful picture of life in London I do not suppose I would have believed it. Suppose I were to go back to Delhi now and tell another, 'Over there life was very hard.' He would reply, 'Why do you chatter rubbish to us? You have been so prosperous yourself and you are jealous in case we may become the same. That is why you talk like that to discourage us.' But if that man were to come here and see things for himself he would no doubt complain to me, 'Why did you not warn me that life in England was going to be difficult?' And if I retorted, 'I told you so, but you did not listen,' he would say, 'Yes, but how could I understand? I did not believe the truth you told.' In India a man who has been abroad is like a man who has slept and relates his dreams to a hearer. How can he give any idea of what he saw in his sleep to another, and how can the other see what the sleeper himself saw? Only through seeing things with our own eyes can we ever know the truth – and in the end only experience teaches what is correct and what is false. But at that time I had never been outside India. How could I know in advance what sort of experience I was to have in London?

Chapter 21

LEAVING INDIA

I DID not ask my father for permission to go to England. I had lived independently for many years and had qualified in my trade so I felt that I was competent to judge what was best. I was confident that I would do well in England. But my parents were not against my going even though they were naturally sad at my departure, especially my mother. They knew as well as I did that, as we had no land or property, my fortune lay wherever I could get a job with the best wages. My brother also wanted to go to England and asked me to send for him if I found a suitable job for him over there. But entry was not

very easy six years ago; it is even harder now, so I don't see
how he could come.

There were few arrangements for me to make before I departed. I had no house or land of my own to dispose of or
attend to and so my preparations for leaving were quickly
complete.

All the members of my household came to see me off at the
airport – my wife, the children, my brother Baldev and his
family. All the friends I had made at work turned up also. After
all, I had worked for sixteen years in that place, and sixteen
years is no short time, so I knew almost everybody there. They
even put a garland of flowers round my neck before I boarded
the plane. I had very little luggage, just my clothes and a warm
quilt to sleep in.

And so I set off, full of hopes; it never occurred to me to
think how far I was going from my family, or whether I should
miss them or not when I arrived. My mind was filled only with
optimistic thoughts for my future.

Chapter 22

A CRUEL WELCOME

WHEN I arrived in the evening at London airport I looked
around to see who had come to meet me. I saw all the people
who had travelled on the same plane as myself collect their
luggage one by one, go outside and drive off in taxis and cars.
Everyone seemed to have some friend or relative to meet them.
Surely some government official must appear at any moment
and take me to wherever I was to be accommodated? You see,
I was under the impression that if the government issued me a
voucher, this meant that they would make all the arrangements
for my work and accommodation, just as when I was a soldier
the army made all the arrangements as to where we were to go

and what we were to do. Surely, I thought, the government must need electrical workers or they would not have issued a voucher to me. Maybe they are laying electrical cables between England and France, or maybe they need men for maintenance work in their offices. Or else they will train us for whatever work they want us to do, like they did in the army. At all events, they are sure to send someone to meet us from the plane. I did not understand that the voucher was only a permit to work in England and did not assure me of anything more than the right to enter the country.

I kept on waiting and still no one called me. It was raining and quite dark outside although it was summer time, and I felt cold. I had left the heat of Delhi only that morning. 'What sort of place is this where I have landed myself now?' I thought. I looked about me and saw that there were only two other men left of my fellow passengers. They were apparently in the same plight as myself. We started to talk to each other. One had been a school-teacher in India and the other was a young lad of eighteen or so, but both had come like myself expecting to find work in England. None of us could speak much English and we were sitting there helplessly in what seemed like a kind of courtyard. Our luggage had been placed there for us to collect after the customs had inspected it and it seemed that we had been left there to die since it became clear that no one was going to turn up to meet us. Around us there was the usual bustle which goes on at an airport, people running to and fro, dancing about on their own business and taking no notice of us. So we began to discuss what we ought to do. Knowing no English, whom should we ask and how? We had not even any idea of the customs of the place, where we could go to buy a meal or how we could ask for accommodation for the night, nor could we see any Indian among the airport officials whom we could approach. We were in a tough spot, and all I could think was, 'Dear God, please get me out of this mess.'

Now none of us had more than three pounds in cash upon him so I said, 'Let us go through our pockets and see if one of us has some acquaintance's address. Then we can pool our

money to pay for a taxi and all go there for to night at least.'
The school-master was the first to come across an address. He
produced an old envelope which had contained a letter from a
fellow villager now living in England. This friend had written
his address on the back of his letter, but we were not even sure
whether we would be able to pronounce it correctly to the taxi
driver. The first taxi-driver we called could not understand our
attempts to pronounce it at all and drove away unable to help
us. The second one was not sure whether the name we were
trying to say was the surname of the man we wanted to visit or
the name of the road he lived in, but when we produced the
envelope and showed it to him he managed to make out the
address and told us that he would take us there. We stowed all
our luggage in the taxi and sat down inside, feeling very relieved. The address we had given was in East London, but we
did not know London and had no idea that it would be such a
long way from the airport. It seemed that we had been in the
taxi for at least an hour and we began to get worried. We asked
each other what could be the matter. Where was the man taking us? Perhaps he intended to take us to some lonely place,
then beat us up and rob us. After all, he was not to know that
none of us had much money in his pocket. There would be no
witness to the crime and as we did not know the language we
could not even ask for help. But just as we were discussing
what we ought to do in this dilemma, the taxi slowed down
and stopped before a house. The school-master's friend ran
out of the house and was obviously delighted at his arrival. He
even paid the driver. He welcomed us in also. He sat us down
and made us a cup of tea, and as I drank it I looked about me
and thought how different this house was from those I had
been used to in India. The chairs, beds, doors and windows
were all of unfamiliar design and seemed very strange to me.

We stayed the night there and the next morning I began to
consider where I should go next. Then I remembered that I
had with me a letter, which I had received some time before
my departure, from a fellow villager of mine who had been
living in England for some time. He lived in Birmingham and

he had written to me, 'Do not come to my home straight from the airport. It is a long way from London and if you get a taxi it will cost you a lot of money.' Of course I do not know much about the geography of England now, and I knew even less then, so had he not told me I should not have known that Birmingham was a long way from London. Anyway he had told me the address of an acquaintance of his in London and suggested that I look him up when I arrived. Had I not been so confused the previous night or had I not fallen in with my two companions, I expect it would have occurred to me to try to find this man in the first place. The address I had been given was also in East London so I explained to our host what I wanted to do and asked him if he would be so kind as to accompany me there, for I had no idea how to reach the place. He took me to the right address and left me with the man my friend in Birmingham had told me of. But this man turned out to be a real bastard. First of all he hardly gave me a gracious welcome. 'What have you come for?' he said. He did not even have the grace to say first, 'Come inside, sit down. We are pleased to see you.' No, all he said was, 'What have you come for? You can't stay here. Don't you know that I have only one room?' Well, I had not intended to bother him for accommodation, only to ask him for help in setting me on my feet, so I felt very hurt. Then he went on to say, 'What did you want to come to London for, anyway? I am a draughtsman and I have been out of work for eleven months, so what sort of job do you think you will be able to get, who are quite uneducated? Do you want to spend a year looking for work?' I replied, 'Well, I did not know anything about this when I came. I thought that the voucher ensured my employment. In any case our friend in Birmingham had told me that jobs were easily found. Perhaps you could take me to him and I could find a job in Birmingham.' 'That will be a waste of time,' he said. 'I was up in Birmingham myself only last week and I am sorry to say that our friend recently lost his job too. It is no use bothering him. If he can't keep the job he has had for six years, do you think you are likely to be able to find one?' This made me even more depressed because in India when a man is out of work it may be years before he can get a job again. That fellow so discouraged me that I felt as though my ship had truly sunk. I began to think that England was evidently not as I had thought it to be, not as it had been described to me. Why did no one tell me of all these problems, I thought? Surely those who had encouraged me to go should have warned me of these difficulties. How could I hope to get work if this was really the situation? Of course work is not really so hard to find, but I was not to know that when I had only just arrived. That man just wanted to discourage me and get rid of me as soon as he could.

Fortunately I found another address in my pocket, that of another fellow villager. He was a Jat and had owned land in our village. I had been unwilling to turn to him in the first place because I had known him in India and knew that he was a scoundrel. But now I was in such despair that I decided I had better call on him as a last resort. So I asked the man I had stayed with to show me the way to where he lived, in West London. He told me that he would take me there and I left his house with relief. That was the last I saw of him, and up to this day he has never troubled to find out what became of me in the end. No one ever said to me, 'We saw so-and-so the other day and he was asking if we knew what had happened to the chap who once spent a night at his place.'

I was not made any more welcome at the Jat's house. When I arrived he said to me, 'Well, Rampal, what do you want? Are you going to stay here or to go back with him?' (Meaning the man who had brought me.) I had expected at least a more gracious greeting than this. After all we both came from the same place and his mother was *dharmbahin* to my mother. He was a son of my village. But he was most unwilling to put me up. So I said to him, 'The thing is, I have no one else here to turn to. Tell me, what can I do, sir? I have only three pounds on me and no job. I know now that I made a great mistake in leaving a job where I earned plenty and a house which only cost me four rupees a month. I was not badly off. But now I have made this mistake and it is too late to go back, because I have given in my notice where I worked in Delhi and have no money for my fare. Everything has gone wrong and I need your help.'

Well, his wife and brother were with him and I heard him consulting them behind the door, 'What shall we do with him?' he asked them. 'Oh, put him to work cooking the food,' said his brother. So he agreed to let me stay for a while provided that I earned my keep by helping them in the kitchen. This is the kind of experience that has made me disappointed in people. Suppose you have some feeling for me and come to me when you are in trouble. Suppose you say to me, 'I am in difficulties. Please tell me what to do.' How will you feel if I just brush you off? That man just treated me like a low-caste beggar. Those from whom I had hoped for assistance gave me no comfort, only humiliation and bitterness.

Chapter 23

EARLY DAYS IN ENGLAND

My next problem was to find myself some work. At first I was so lonely and miserable that I thought, 'At least let me earn my own fare home and I will return to India as soon as possible.' Later I began to settle down and I realised that it would be better to save money and bring my family over to join me, but in the early days I just prayed that I might be able to earn enough to catch a plane home again. I was not long out of work however. One day an Indian visiting the house where I lived happened to mention that I might be able to get a job at the factory opposite his house. They needed electricians there, he said, and it might be worth my while to apply. He took me to see the manager and explained that I had only just arrived from India. The manager told us to come again the next day for an interview. The next day we went again and I got the job. Of course, I had only studied a few grades at school and my English was very weak; I just about knew the difference between 'yes' and 'no'. My companion explained to the manager, 'My friend does not know much English but he is a qualified electrician. If anything goes wrong he can mend it, he really knows what's what.' So the manager said that he would test me. 'What is this?' he asked. 'Armature,' I said. 'What is this?' 'This is a switch,' I answered. The manager was satisfied and said that they would have me. Wasn't this proof of God's power, that my prayer was fulfilled so quickly? I was so grateful to that manager for agreeing to take me on that I regarded him as my benefactor and food-giver. Later I found that he was hardly worthy of so much respect. For one thing he did not treat coloured people well, for another he fiddled his income tax and knew all sorts of other tricks. He was a real crook. But I was desperate to get work at that time and he seemed to have answered my prayers. He could have said anything he liked to me and I would still have looked upon him as my own kin.

I quite liked the work I had to do in that factory although I did not always get on with the people there, and I changed my job two years later and went to work in the Ministry of Works. Those early days in England were most miserable for me. I hardly like to speak of the time.

When they first come to this country, different types of men react in different ways to their new experiences. One type of man, the kind who is very unsophisticated and perhaps not very intelligent – he is quite thick-skinned. He is happy in England because he earns twopence and eats twopence. He is not sensitive to what anyone says. If people abuse him or let him down he reflects no further upon it! 'I have neither to marry nor to give in marriage in this country,' he thinks. 'My honour does not lie in this country that I may lose it here. If I die, I die. If I live, I live.' He is happy here and when he goes back to India he no doubt boasts to his relatives. They are proud of him and show him off to their neighbours in turn.

He quickly forgets any difficulties which he encounters; they soon pass from his mind.

And then there is the other type of man, the type to which I belong, who cannot accept every setback or hurt with equanimity. He questions his suffering and says to himself, 'What am I to do? Why does this happen to me?' This is how it was with me, and my pain was deepened by these thoughts. Firstly I was terribly lonely. I had been let down and treated like dirt by the people to whom I had turned for help. 'If only I had some relative or true friend here,' I thought. 'They would surely come to my aid.' But I had no one. I was hurt and alone in a strange country. I was so lonely that if I met any Indian in the street I would try to talk to him. At that time there were fewer Indians here than there are now; sometimes I would approach someone I thought to be an Indian and address him in Punjabi. But he would turn out to be Ceylonese – Ceylonese are very like Indians to look at – and of course would not understand me at all. Then I would be the more deeply disappointed.

Most of all I missed my family. 'My children must be yearning to see me over there, and here am I yearning to see them,' I thought. I started to put money away in the post office every week, thinking that if only I could save enough to bring my family over to join me I might after all be happy in this country. And then if only I could save enough money to buy a house so that I was not dependent on the good will of landlords, we might get out of our straits altogether. But I could not earn much money at first. I knew that I could earn more if I did a labourer's job and put in as much overtime as I could, but my stamina has never been so great that I could wield heavy weights every day. My body has never been very strong and now I was getting weaker with worry. I began to think that I had been a fool to leave the job that I had enjoyed in Delhi. There I had earned only Rs. 160 a month but I had led a joyous life. There I had lived in poverty but I had always had faith that whatever I delighted in, God would give it me in the end. In India I had seen people eat from golden platters, employing hundreds of servants to run after them, their every wish attended to by others, but I had never envied them. I had not longed for material things so much as for freedom from worry about practical matters. Nor have I changed now; I am still a man of humble tastes. I only wish for a peaceful and secure life. If I could earn more money, I had thought when I was in Delhi, I would never need to trouble myself about our future. I would be free from these worries. But now I had come to England at last I was more worried than before. I had thought that my family's fare could be earned in a few weeks' work and now I had come so far only to find that it would take months, even years, for me to earn so much. I wondered why I had ever grumbled about poverty in India. After all, men can live happily on bread and water. If God provides salt and spices as well, then taste them by all means, but we should not fall into the trap of thinking these are essentials too.

For months I hardly slept and my weight fell by at least a stone in that time. I felt that I had fallen from human state. 'I have only a few more breaths to draw in this world,' I thought. 'There is no cure for my misery now.' If a man has terrible pain in some part of his body, what will he reply if you ask him how he feels? He will be aware only of that pain, and nothing else will he be able to speak of. Or if an old man of seventy has only one son and that son dies, is there anything left in his heart to hope for? In either case the man feels that to live and to die is all one. He is consumed by his distress. No other question can distract his mind, once he reached the stage where he feels that there is no cure for his suffering. That is the state in which I found myself. There was no one to whom I could tell my pain yet nor could I hold it back in my heart. All day I would spend working hard, and when I came back at night I would just lie down and pull the quilt over my head. I would take a sleeping draught and somehow struggle through the night, hoping to find some relief in unconsciousness until it was morning and time to go to work again. That is how the time passed with me for many months.

Chapter 24

'YOU MUST KNOW ENGLISH'

W HEN I first started work at that factory I was the only Indian employed there. Other Indians came to work there later but at that time I was alone. I did not know much English and so I felt very lonely. I used to think how good it would be if some fellow countryman of mine were to come and work alongside me, some educated Indian who would aid and encourage me. He would help me to learn English and explain things to me. But there was no one and I had to manage alone.

So far as my work was concerned, it was not really necessary to know much English. My job was electrical maintenance work and if the light goes out you don't need to understand English to know that it has fused. If the heating system does not function and the place is freezing you don't need a degree in English to know that something is amiss. You just look at the machinery with your own eyes and see why it has come to a standstill, and then put it right.

But in other matters I badly needed help with the language. You must know English if you are to remain in this country. Suppose my children fall sick and I have to take them to the hospital. How can I explain what is wrong if I do not know the language? Most Indians solve this problem by trying to find an Indian doctor for themselves. Educated Indians may take on an English doctor, but those who are unlettered like us will search around for an Indian one, even if they have to trudge four or five miles to find one. Because only to a fellow-countryman can they explain all their ills in their own language. But suppose they are unable to find an Indian doctor, then they will look for some educated Indian who is willing to accompany them to their English doctor's house. He can interpret for them, both in this and in other matters. For instance, when my family came over here to join me and I had to enrol the children in school, I took an Indian acquaintance who had some education along with me and he explained everything to the headmaster. And then he would tell me what the headmaster said. That is how Indians manage when they don't know much English.

Now I understand quite a lot of English, at least I can speak a little. I can read English even better than I speak it. I understand written English fairly well.

It is not really so much to my credit that I have learnt so quickly. No matter what country you find yourself in, if you have to live alongside its people you automatically pick up their language. Suppose you go to Africa and stay there some time – slowly, slowly, you will come to understand what the people there say. After four or five years you will have a good knowledge of their language. That is how it was with me; through working with English people and living amongst them I came to understand their tongue.

Chapter 25

SATYA TAKES A JOB

AFTER about a year, my wife and children came to join me at last. How happy I was on the day when I realised that I had enough in my savings account to pay for their fares to England! After a year of saving I had sufficient money at last, and I was so relieved to have them with me again. Our next objective was to buy our own house here so that we could live independently and would not have to rely on others to give us accommodation. Therefore I suggested to Satya that she take a job in the factory where I worked, so that we could save more money.

In that factory they used to treat aluminium goods. Machine

parts made of aluminium would be sent from some other factory to be anodysed, coloured and assembled, and many women were employed in this work. For instance, a thousand or more rings would arrive, tied in one dozen bundles, and the women would colour them and put them together. It was light work and not at all difficult. Some jobs were harder – in the same factory they employed women packing – but I got my wife a job in the assembling department because that was not such heavy work.

It worked very well because her table was right near the door which I had to pass through in order to get to my room. So I was always around to explain to her what she had to do. All the other women there were either English or Jamaican and the charge-hand was English too. The charge-hand would tell me what work she must do and I would explain to her in Punjabi. Then they would leave her to it, to finish it at her own pace. But she has always been a quick worker and that is why they were always pleased with her at the factory. Satya gets on well with English people because they like a woman to be a hard worker. They don't care whether a woman is pretty or not, whether or not she has a pleasant manner of talking, whether or not she is smart. In fact they would rather have a woman who puts on less lipstick and gets through more work. The more work she does the better, be she never so plain. So Satya always got on well there because she just gets on with her task.

There was another reason why I liked her to work there. She was the only Indian woman there when she first started work there. Had she been in the midst of a crowd of Indian women they might have picked quarrels with her. They might have been jealous of her, or tried to show off, as though they were better than she. Indians are like that. They are jealous of each other and each wants the other to be under his thumb. If one starts a new job at a factory, the Indian who was already there wants the newcomer to take orders from him alone. The orders really come from the charge-hand but he tries to give the impression that they come from him. If the new man does not flatter him and make him feel important then he will try to get him turned out of the place. This has happened to me, so I know from my own experience. He will tell tales about him and play some trick on him. That is an Indian's first job when another Indian comes to join him at his place of work, and the women are just the same. So I was glad that there were no Indian women already working in our factory at that time who could give Satya trouble of that kind. Even if she were bothered by anyone, I was there to keep an eye on things. We were the only Indians there and no one troubled us. They just left us alone to complete our work as we wished. In fact when other Indians came to join us there, it was we who had found them their jobs. One or two women asked us to recommend them for jobs with Satya. They left later but others came to take their places. Gradually more and more came, but it was we who started it off. As I was to discover, it was a very great mistake on our part to put other Indians to work beside us, but I did not realise that while I was alone there. I only longed to have other fellow-countrymen for company.

Chapter 26

'WHERE WILL I GO IF I LOSE THIS JOB?'

I T is my experience that there are few good men in this world. Many will say, 'You are a grand fellow,' but few will mean it or feel sincerely glad to see you prosper. When you hear what happened to me later at that factory you will agree in your heart and say, 'What this Rampal is telling me is quite true.'

After I had worked in the factory for nearly two years an Indian by the name of Mohan Singh, whom I knew a little, asked me to find him a job there. I introduced him to the manager and he succeeded in getting work as a charge-hand in the anodysing department. I was working as an electrician at that time. Soon after he started work he told me that his brother needed a job also. His brother was also an electrician by trade. So Mohan Singh said to me, 'Why don't you come and work in the anodysing department along with me? I am the charge-hand there so I can get you transferred. Then my brother can take your place as electrician. What difference does it make to you anyway where you work, so long as you are allowed to carry on with it in peace? It is the money that counts.' I said, 'Very well, we two will be able to work alongside each other then.' I was transferred to his department and began to work under him.

Now we ought to have got along well together, oughtn't we? I had got him a job in the first place, so just as I had helped him he should have been ready to help me. There should have been harmony and affection between us. But after a few months I found that we were not getting along well at all. Perhaps it was just because he was indebted to me that he resented me, but we could not work together with any love for each other. He quickly became angry and impatient if I made the slightest mistake. At first I thought, 'Never mind, we will soon get used to each other.' But this was not the case, and things became worse. Then I discovered that what he wanted was to turn me out of this job also. A friend of his needed work and he thought that if he could get me sacked his friend could take my place. He had already got his brother a job in the factory and now he wanted his friend to be there also, even if he were to get his own way at my expense, although I did not realise this at the time.

When we had completed one batch of goods we had to stack them ready to be taken away. One day I saw him pick one out from the pile and deliberately throw it on the ground. That morning he said to me, 'Rampal, you are no worker, look what you have done.' Of course the parts that he himself had dropped had got scratched. Any goods which were scratched had to be put aside and repainted. Then there would be a lot of fuss and abuse for the fellow who had done it, just because a few goods

had been damaged. Even though I had done no wrong and it
was he who really damaged the parts, he went to the works
manager and complained that I was incapable of doing the
work properly. Now should he not have returned the kindness
which I had shown him when I got him the job and then agreed
to change my work to make a place for his brother? Should he
not have been content with that? Even if I had really been
careless or clumsy couldn't he have said, 'Never mind, it does
not matter. What has been broken can always be mended
again.' No matter what I did, he was always angry with me. To
this day I have never understood why I allowed myself to eat
his insults for so long. I accepted such humiliation only because
I was anxious to keep the job. I feared to complain lest I should
find myself without work again.

Mohan Singh was very thick with the works manager and so
when he told him that Rampal was no good and it was no use
keeping him, the manager agreed. Mohan Singh came to me
that day and said to me, 'You are getting two weeks' notice.
You had better look for another job.' Tell me, what do you
think of that? It was all underhand. If we had been in India
people would just have said, 'They could not get along together and they quarrelled.' Because we were both immigrants
we had to find excuses. I asked him why I was being dismissed
and he said, 'The manager was angry that you asked him for a
rise. He took it very badly and now he doesn't want to see your
face around here. You had better make some other arrangement for yourself.' The fact was that I had asked for a rise the
previous week. I had felt that the time had come when I needed
more money than I was getting.

My family had arrived here and we were applying for a
mortgage to buy the house. I had taken all the forms the building society had sent us to show to the works manager and I
explained the whole matter to him. 'I have worked here for
nearly three years,' I said, 'and I am established in this job. I
only need a little more money so that we can afford to buy our
house.' The manager had said that he would consider my case.
And now I was being given two weeks' notice just for that!

Everything had gone wrong; now that my job had gone, how would I be able to get the house? I said to Mohan Singh, 'If that is all I am being fired for, I can always go to the office and tell them that I don't want a rise after all. Is my notice really final? Is there no hope for me?' 'No hope at all,' he said, 'It is absolutely final.' Then I suggested to him that we go together to the general manager's office and appeal to him. 'You could tell him that you want me to be kept on, that I have been working under you for some time, that my work was quite satisfactory,' I said. Now he was caught. He had only said that I was being fired for asking for a rise so that I would not know that it was his deceit that had got me dismissed. He was passing the buck and did not want to take responsibility for what he had done. It was then that I tumbled to the fact that the very man I had been working with had tricked me and I was very angry. I challenged him, 'Come to the manager with me and I will tell him in front of you the way I have been treated.' He refused to come and said that it was a matter for the works manager and the general manager to settle between themselves. How could he act contrary to their authority, he asked? I had had enough of this man and was in despair as to what I should do now. How would I ever get such a good job again, when not only was I an immigrant to this country but not even tough in physique so that I could take on a labouring job? I told him straight out, 'I have had enough of you. Give me notice, would you? Go and fuck your sister if you have got one to fuck. You have been asking for this abuse and now you are getting it.' That is what I said, standing right there in front of him. Usually I do not swear or lose my temper, but I had been submissive for too long and could stand no more. I was at the end of my tether.

That Friday after work I went to the works manager's house myself and explained the whole matter to him, how Mohan Singh had intended to get his friend appointed in my place, and how he had contrived to get me dismissed. There was another reason why Mohan Singh had disliked me, which was that I had refused to clock in for him and his friends when they came on the late bus. Why should I risk my job when I was only a visitor in this country and would certainly have difficulty in finding another? I told this to the manager also. I think the manager had had some idea of what had been going on and he said to me, 'Rampal, I can see that it is no good your working alongside this man. I will see that you are transferred to another plant.' The following Friday I was due to receive my cards so I was rather surprised that I was being shifted around at this point, but I felt that perhaps there was some hope. Yet I did not hear anything more. On my last day I was frantic with worry as to where I should go or what I should do next. At mid-day I went home for lunch and when I returned I saw Mohan Singh at the gates of the factory and the manager was standing somewhere behind him. But I did not heed the manager, I was so angry with Mohan Singh. I went up to him and asked him, 'Well, did you fuck your sister like I told you to? Would you have me turned out then?' I made a great mistake in abusing him just then, because the manager heard me and he came forward and said, 'I had realised that you had done nothing wrong before, but if it is your nature to swear at other people, Rampal, then you must go. I do not want any fighting here!' He knew that to-day might pass without a fight so long as he was standing around, but to-morrow we would certainly have come to blows. He was right, because at that time I was quite ready to take on both Mohan Singh and his brother, tough though they were. I had the feeling that Mohan Singh must have got at the manager behind my back and that the manager must have preferred to believe his word rather than mine. Anyway, whether or not he had really been ready to consider keeping me on before this incident, now that I had abused Mohan Singh he was certainly determined to get rid of me, and I was forced to leave after all.

As it turned out, I was fortunate enough to find my present job at the Ministry of Works without much trouble, even though I had been afraid that I would be out of work for a long time. So eventually we were able to buy our house after all. But I was very bitter at the treatment I had received. An

Englishman can feel secure in his job, for this is his country. If he is pushed around he can say to the foreman, 'What do you think I am?' If there is any to-do, he can answer back. But an Indian like myself thinks, 'Where will I go if I lose this job?' and is more cautious than is good for him.

Chapter 27

'A GREAT PROBLEM FOR ME'

MORE than any other problem in this country I have felt my lack of good friends to turn to for help and encouragement. Instead of friendship I have too often met with ill treatment and deception from others. I have no real English friends. Of course I get on fairly well with the English people I work with and I have many English acquaintances who seem to like me well enough – people like my next door neighbours, for instance, or the manager of the bank where I have my account. But I have never been able to make any deep friendship with an English person. How can I make friends with English people when my knowledge of their language is so poor? And in any case, how can I expect English people to want to be friendly with me when they are always busy with their own affairs? It is their own country and they are amongst their own people, so why should I expect them to come running to my help?

At the factory where I worked after I first arrived in England, I had a great regard for the foreman who was my superior. I wanted very much to make friends with him. But he seemed to have no regard for me. I am the kind of man who quickly becomes hurt by the criticism of a friend. Sometimes I make mistakes and people who have no patience would call me a fool. But surely, if you are friends with a person you will be ready to tolerate their small faults? You don't slap them in the face every time they stumble. If they break something, can't it be mended again? There is no need to become angry about it. Perhaps he thought me stupid but that foreman did not seem to want to return my friendship at all, and just brushed me off.

The manager who first gave me the job in that factory was the Englishman whom I held in the highest esteem at that time. I felt real affection for him because he had helped me by giving me work. When my wife and children came here to join me I took them to visit him at his house once or twice. His wife took quite a fancy to my little daughter Asha and used to give her pennies to spend. But he himself did not seem to want my friendship. I had the feeling that he was always aware that I was coloured and could not bring himself to feel affection for a coloured man, no matter how much love that coloured man had for him.

As for Indians, I have made a few friends amongst those that I have met over here. The only man I care for much is a second cousin of mine who lives quite near to us here in London. He is my father's cousin's son. His son-in-law came to England some years ago and then sent for his wife to join him. My cousin also decided to come along with his daughter and got work here. But he obtained entry as his son-in-law's dependant; he did not come on a voucher as I did. When we had both been living in India we had not been particularly close to each other. He was one of a big family and had many friends and relatives, whereas I was almost alone. And what use has a man surrounded by his own kin for a man who has no one? He is in no need for friendship so he does not worry about others. All the same, a few months after I came here he sent me a letter telling me that he had just arrived in England and informing me of his address, so of course I had to go and visit him. How glad and relieved I was to see him! There is no doubt that, however deep a man's distress, some peace comes from seeing someone he can call his own. It does not matter whether they are his from being of the same family, through coming from the same district, the same cast or the same village. When you see someone of your own blood you feel, 'Now everything will be all right.' There is a natural attraction to your own kin, and to have someone who belongs to you is more important than money or possessions. So when I met my cousin after so many months of loneliness, I felt great relief and comfort. Since then we have visited him quite frequently, and he has visited us.

Apart from this, I cannot say that I have found much friendship among other Indians. Although no one gave me any help when I was new here, I have done things for so many other Indians, helping them to find jobs or accommodation. Yet none of them has shown me gratitude or affection.

I know that I am a simple man and I ought to be more firm with other people so that they will never mistreat me. My character is like that of the simple snake. When God created the snake he said to him, 'Brother snake, all the world fears you, therefore you must be gentle and not bite anyone.' So the snake never troubled anyone with the result that everyone abused him. They used him as a rope to tie bundles of firewood or a string for hanging up their water vessels on the wall. Everyone thought, 'This snake does not know how to defend himself, you can do anything with him.' The poor snake's body was scratched and broken, bleeding in many places. So he went to God and said, 'Father, people will not let me live in peace. Look, they have used me as a rope.' God replied to him, 'Silly snake, I told you not to bite people, but I never said you were not to hiss at them.' I am like that simple snake because I too do not know how to make myself appear tough. I know that people take advantage of me, thinking that I am soft, but I do not know how to prevent it from happening again. For instance, the other day some Indian neighbours came here to ask for a loan of fifty pounds. It was to help some relative of theirs to come to this country. Now what was I to do? I find it hard to say 'no' to people. I do not like to lie, but people force me to lie. I said that I would try to give them some money by the weekend, but I don't really want to. I need all the money I can earn and who knows whether they would return the loan? I live frugally; you know that I don't drink or smoke, nor do I have any girl friends. We try to save money on little things, buying clothes in sales when we can. We spend no more than is essential and send money to our relatives in India from time to time as well as saving for ourselves. I never once took a loan, or any article on hire purchase. Now, do I live frugally just so that others can enjoy the fruits of my economy? Yet I never know what to say when people ask me for money or to do things for them. It is a great problem for me.

Chapter 28

BEING COLOURED (1)

I THINK that there is more race prejudice since Africa became independent when so many Indian people arrived here from over there.[1] Before that time English people were more friendly to us and would talk to us more willingly. But when large numbers of Indians started to arrive from Africa, then I noticed some difference in their attitude to us. They seemed to feel: 'It was not like this before. There are too many Indians here now. They are wandering about all over our country.'

Or course it is difficult for me to tell whether the English people I meet treat me differently from their own people. For instance, where I work, I am the only Indian at present, so it is difficult for me to judge whether they treat me the way they do because of my colour or whether they would treat me like that even if I were white. If there were, say, five or ten Indians besides myself working there, then I might notice some difference between the way they behaved towards Indians and the way they behaved amongst themselves. It would be possible to tell from the way in which they addressed us and from the manner in which they spoke to us.

1. Rampal is referring to the expulsion of many Indians from Kenya in 1967.

93

Formerly, I did not notice that people were specially aware of my colour. But lately, now that there are so many Indians here, the people I work with have begun to express quite openly some dislike for coloured people. Before, they never used to say anything to me but now they ask me, 'What do you people come here for?' If I make any remark about England, comparing it with India in any respect, they just say, 'Why don't you go back home then?' For instance, if I ask them why they like going to pubs and what attraction there is for them in drinking, they say, 'We like to go, it is our way of life,' and they laugh at me for not going myself. They tell me that as I have come here I ought to conform to their ways, and if I do not go to dances and clubs then I am in the wrong. 'You people should do these things too,' they say. 'Otherwise what have you come here for?' Or if I say that in India we do not like to see a man and a woman kissing each other on the street, they say, 'Then you people are mistaken. You should do as we do.' Of course when we are in England we should not offend English people – it is their country, not ours. Yet if we were to force them to conform to our customs in India they would not like it. All the white-skinned people I have met in this country regard Indians and Jamaicans as beneath them. They see them as an alien kind. When they have their Trades Union meetings and so forth, they do not count us, nor are they interested in helping our causes. Still, I suppose it is understandable. It is only the same as the way in which high-caste people do not count the low-castes. The high-caste people do not count the low-caste people as of their own kind and therefore they do not feel any desire to help them. High-caste people do not want to form any kind of social relationship with low-caste people if they can help it. Here it is a matter of colour, there a matter of caste; if there is any difference it is only one of degree.

I do not think my wife or children have ever been mistreated because of their colour; the children have never complained to me that anyone has ever called them black and they seem to be well treated at school. But I myself know what

English people are thinking and saying, because there are many English people where I work and I hear them talking about these things all the time.

I know that one of the main ways in which English people show that they do not like coloured people is in the matter of accommodation. I myself have never had the experience of being rejected by an English landlord, but that is because I have never applied to one for rooms. I never applied because I am a family man and I know from other Indians that English people do not like tenants with children. A husband and wife alone they are prepared to take, but not a couple with a family. When my wife and children first came here we lived in two rooms let to us by some Indians who owned a shop. After we left that place, we lived in one room in the house of some Indians from British Guiana for a few months. Then we spent a short while in the *gurudvara*, and after that we rented two rooms from another Indian family, sharing the kitchen with them. As we have never lived with an English landlord I cannot say what sort of treatment they mete out to their coloured tenants. One should not relate what one has merely heard from others as it may be false, so I am only telling you what I have seen with my own eyes.

I suppose that one of the reasons why English people do not like Indian tenants must be that they do not like the smell of our food. We put a lot of spices in our cooking – chillies, turmeric, coriander – and so it is inevitable that it will smell, isn't it? Whether you think of it as a fine scent or as a foul odour, it is bound to get into the other rooms of the house a little. I once asked an Englishman at the place where I work about this, and he said that he would never want to rent a room to Indians because they prepare such smelly foods and then the smell spreads all over the house unless you install fans everywhere. I remember one of my Indian acquaintances joking with me that the Englishman lavishes the same sort of care upon his house and his car that we Indians lavish on our wives and children. The house and the car are the two things he cares about most. He takes so much thought for the state of his house – all the time he is attending to it – and that is why he forbids Indians to live in it. Therefore Indians live among Indians and English people go to Englishmen.

I am the kind of man who must reflect upon what he sees and hears, and I often wonder in my heart why English people do not think well of coloured people. It really is a matter of colour, because they do not feel the same way towards white foreigners. Those who have the right coloured skins never get stopped at the airport, they just show their passports and go straight through. No one asks whether they are of good or bad character. White foreigners who come here to work have nothing to fear; their skin is the right colour and so there is no danger for them. Suppose I had come not from India but from France or Holland or Germany. Then no one would tell me to clear off. I would still be a foreigner, wouldn't I? But no one would abuse me. My children are being brought up here, but they will think of themselves as Indian and will live as Indians because so long as their colour is not white, English people will not regard them as British. A coloured man is easily picked out just because he is coloured. His skin tells you who he is when you are still far from him. If only the government could pass some law to change the colour of people's skin or the scientists would invent some drug to make either all the coloured people white or all white people coloured, then perhaps all would be well. But our colour is different and it cannot be changed.

English people fear that coloured people are coming here to eat their money and consume their country. The man in the social security office sits behind his desk and watches Indians coming to apply for family allowances or sickness benefits and thinks, 'I have been paying tax for so many years. Was it just to provide free food for these people with their six children apiece?' (That is what people say, isn't it?) He feels real pain when he gives them money, for the idea has lodged in his brain that they are not entitled to it. He forgets that as long as they work over here they also pay tax to the government.

Then there is the matter of numbers. Only a certain number

of people can live in a house together, not more. If the floor is only made with the strength to support the weight of ten men and you stand fifteen men upon it, then it will collapse. The Englishman is afraid that his house is going to be over-crowded like that. In our country there is land attached to certain temples, sometimes as much as five hundred acres. The priest who looks after the temple must remain celibate but adopts one disciple to succeed him as guardian of the temple and its estates. The land and the priesthood will pass to that man alone upon his death. He is the only heir and so the land remains undivided. But suppose the priest were allowed to marry. He might have five, ten or even more sons. The land is divided amongst them and each has only one hundred acres. Children are born in the houses of each of the five sons and the land is divided again. It goes on being divided with each generation until the inheritance of each heir is so small that it is hardly worth having. Unless some limit is imposed by law, that wealth is finished. In the same way, English people fear that if hundreds of thousands of people come to share their country there will be nothing left for them. Once they were rich, they ruled over so many countries; now they have lost their power. There is no one in this world who does not want his own people to prosper, even at the expense of others, so must they not feel bitter in their hearts?

Chapter 29

'THIS IS NOT OUR COUNTRY'

I HAVE always said that this is not our country and we are here as guests. There is much difference between the ways of Indians and the ways of English people, but if we are to stay here we must to some extent do as the English wish. Only then will there be happiness between us all. It is no use Indians coming here and demanding everything as their rightful due. Suppose someone were to come to my house and tell me, 'Don't touch that, put your shoes here, do as I say,' or even, 'This is my house, you must get out,' would I like it? Therefore if we are to remain here we must work and earn our money in an orderly way and behave ourselves decently. Any Indian who is prepared to do this should be allowed to stay, and anyone who is not must go home. The land belongs to those who are born there and it is their inheritance.

There are many ways in which this could be ensured so that all the people could live in peace with each other, English, Indians and Jamaicans. For one thing, the English government could join with our government to prevent people from coming here illegally. Those travel agents who take money from Indians telling them that they can get them into the country and then do so by cheating and telling lies should be punished severely, indeed anyone who tampers with the laws or twists people in a country where he is a guest deserves to be seized and shot. And if Indians make trouble at work by forming factions and causing disturbances, they should be turned out. Whoever is at fault, there should be strict justice. Of course not all Indians are bad or misbehave; on the contrary many are very good and never break the law. But it is like a man's body. Sometimes one part goes wrong – his hand, his back, his heart – and then the whole body is prevented from doing its work. The man does not feel well or easy in himself. So when a few Indians behave badly they make things difficult for the rest of us, for the whole community. English people are not stupid. They are all educated; there is not one of them who has not attended school for at least ten years. There are no illiterates among them as there are in India. Apart from what they learn at school they gather things about the world from watching television. Therefore they should be able to find some sensible way to solve the race problem justly. They should be able to think of a good way of limiting the numbers of Indians and Jamaicans coming here, for if too many come then relations are spoiled and broken. They should get together and approach the government with some good suggestion as to how this could be accomplished fairly and by law.

It is just because we are guests in this country that I often feel afraid and insecure about staying here. English people will tolerate coloured people here only as long as they need them. Those who are necessary to them have their demands met quickly enough. If I were a doctor or a scientist I would be in a position to ask for things and my requests would probably be met, but people like myself come here as labourers and if we lose our value they will soon tell us to go. They will tell Indian scientists and doctors to go as soon as they no longer need them. The things which you cannot do without are dear to your heart and you will not abuse them readily, but what you do not need you have little regard for. We are vulnerable here because we are insecure and this is humiliating for us, a matter of shame. If the government decides to turn us out, no amount of marching up and down with flags and petitions will do us any good. If the foreman abuses us and fires us, no amount of protest will get us back our jobs. An Englishman can answer back because he knows the language, he can stand up for himself. He does not depend on the good will of others and can easily get another job in any case.

I have seen for myself that those who are in a minority have no strength to bargain. When India was partitioned in 1947, those Hindus who lived in Pakistan had to do what the Muslims wanted, and those Muslims who lived in India had to abide by the will of the Hindus. Hindus and Muslims had lived together in peace until the riots broke out, and then those who were many turned upon those who were few and made them comply with their will. Then it was no use for those in the minority to hope for mercy from those who had been their friends. As the master of the house decreed, so the tenants were obliged to do. From my own experiences at that time, I know how suddenly and quickly political conditions can change, and I feel afraid lest I should see that kind of communal fighting again, this time in England.

I feel the more fearful since it is always difficult to tell what English people really mean. Sometimes they appear very kind and compassionate outwardly but in their hearts are other thoughts. A corn merchant may appear to be very kind, giving thousands of rupees to charity, but in his mind he is thinking, 'Let me hold the rice back a little longer and the price will rise even further.' One can never judge what English people are feeling from what they say and this makes me feel the more insecure. They may seem friendly but in reality resent coloured people. The outward appearance is one thing, the inner intention another. They may not say openly, 'Turn coloured people out of their jobs,' but they might treat them in such a way that they could not tolerate working here any longer.

I do not feel very hopeful about the future of Indians in this country. At present the government is not altogether unfavourable to us.[1] But no Prime Minister or President is in power for ever, and when he falls all those whom he favoured fall as well, automatically. No minority can remain in a country without the consent of the majority unless they have come as conquerors, defending their presence by the sword. Did not the Indians turn out even the English from their country in the end? So we can only stay here so long as the government tolerates us. If a mother is carrying her baby across a deep river, she lifts the child on to her shoulders when the water reaches her chest, and on to her head when the water reaches her shoulders. But when the water covers her face and she drowns then the baby will automatically fall into the water and drown also. Like the baby, we coloured people can only survive in this country so long as the government is willing to support our presence and carry our cause. If those who tolerate us are thrown from power we will also be forced to leave.

I used not to worry about this kind of thing, but since this Powell has been making speeches I have begun to think more about it and to be afraid. I do not take any English newspapers because I cannot read them easily, but I hear about these political matters from my friends and from what I see on tele-

1. This was recorded before the election of June, 1970.

vision. Other Indians I know feel the same. We cannot tell how soon the day will come when we shall be told, 'Now, brothers, it is time for you to go.' If such circumstances were to arise and I were to be left with no money for my return fare, what should I feel? I should feel that I had sacrificed my youth in a foreign land to no purpose. Therefore I am anxious to save as much money as possible against that day. The uncertainty about our future here, the feeling that we might be ordered to leave tomorrow, makes me feel restless about what is to come.

Chapter 30

'ALL HAVE THEIR DIFFERENT WAYS'

MY work companions often ask me about Indian customs, and I have to explain to them that they are very different from English ways. I do not think that they find our habits easy to understand – indeed, why should they? I could not understand how English people lived until I came over here. When I told them that when I got married in the village I had never seen my wife's face, they said, 'What a stupid way of doing things. No one in their senses buys a thing without first looking it over.' How could I convince them that I am very happy and contented in my marriage? I could not make them understand that every man prefers the customs of his own land. I used to ask them, 'Well, tell me how you find your wives then.' They told me that boys and girls meet each other in youth clubs, offices and factories where they work, or in dance halls. I know that this is true, for I have seen it for myself. There are clubs near to where I live, and boys and girls go there regularly. They seek friends amongst themselves. If a boy becomes a member, sooner or later some girl will take a fancy to him. He is sure to find a bride eventually; there is no need for him to go about with a placard hung round his neck to tell

the world that he needs a wife. These clubs bring people together, just as the barber used to do in India. But surely
marriages made in this way will be made impulsively. Can anyone judge another's true nature just from watching him dance?

The other difference is that here every girl is let loose to
wander about as she pleases. In India a young girl does not
even go out for a walk, let alone stay the night anywhere, without her parents' consent. She cannot even look at a man unless
they agree. Here I can approach any pretty girl and ask her to
go out with me, and she will not think ill of me. Indeed, here
girls even approach men themselves. One day I was coming
home from work when one of the Jamaican women from our
factory overtook me at the zebra crossing in the High Street.
(Jamaicans and English – they are all the same so far as these
customs are concerned. Do they not both speak the same
language, after all?) She said to me, 'Hello, Rampal,' so of
course I greeted her in return. But then she said, 'Well, and
when are you going to take me out for a cup of tea?' I was very
embarrassed because I was not sure what she meant or how I
should have replied to such a proposition, so I just looked
down and mumbled something. When I reached home I told
Satya what had happened and she was puzzled too. But then
she joked, 'Oh well, you and I will have to get a divorce just
like English people do.'

And then, look at the people who live next door to us. Their
daughter not only goes out with a boy friend – she even
brings him home. Her mother once said to me, 'She is eighteen
now. She can please herself who she goes with. It is up to her
whether she brings boys home or not.' I wish I understood how
these customs work, yet if I try to discuss them with English
people they just get annoyed and say, 'If you don't care for our
way of life, why don't you go home? If you don't want your
daughters to have boy friends, why do you stay here?' But if
English boys and girls do not like to mix with Indians, how
can our young people mix with them, even if we did approve
of their habits?

Some of the men I work with tell me that they do not want

to get married because they would always be afraid that their wives would be unfaithful to them. And those who are already married are always in fear of displeasing their wives. The trouble seems to be that English women will not tolerate being kept down. The minute anything makes her angry, the English woman says to her husband, 'Get out, there is nothing between us any more.' And it seems that English women demand to be taken everywhere their husbands go. Can this really be so? The English men at work say that their wives grumble if they are not taken out every time they go themselves, whether to clubs, dances or pubs. The Indian boys I know who have married English girls say the same thing. I cannot understand this. Are people in England ruled by their women? Every Englishman seems to have to wait upon his wife and run about after her.

Another difference between English and Indian people is that, whereas in India there are many temples, mosques and churches, English people have no religion now. Few young people go to church, only the old men and women. Many English people even openly profess to have no belief in God and take it very ill if you say to them, 'Brother, it is good to pray.' They say, 'What I believe is my own business; if I want to pray, then I will pray – if not, then I won't.' I suppose that English people have lost their religion because they lack no comforts. They are so well looked after by their government that they neither pray nor save; they take no thought for to-morrow. If the government were to declare that from next week no one would be allowed to draw National Assistance, then they would surely all run to the church to pray to God for help.

Yet another difference that I have noticed between English and Indian people is that people here do not know the meaning of 'sucha' and 'jutha' – pure and defiled. Amongst our Hindu people, no one who is in the middle of eating will touch the water jug or serve himself. We eat with our hands and if your hands have been in your mouth, then they are impure. Even if Hindu people use spoons and forks, they do not dip their spoons into food that other people are going to eat once they have put them into their own mouths. While we are eating, if we need something, then we ask someone who has not yet started his meal or who has already got up and washed his hands to serve us. Any food which has not been touched is kept for another meal, but anything left over is thrown straight into the dustbin. Or it can be given to the birds or animals, because for beasts there is no pure or impure, only for mankind.

English people do not have these concepts of 'pure' and 'impure'. There are not even any words in their language to convey the idea exactly. They only know 'dirty' and 'clean', which are not the same. They put everything on the table and go on helping themselves all the time they are eating. They eat with knives and forks and not with their hands as we do, so it would not matter if they touched things with their hands, but English people are not so particular as we are. If one person is drinking a bottle of orangeade and he says to another, 'Would you like to drink some too?' the other does not retort, 'Why should I drink what you have made impure?' He might refuse it if he did not care for orange juice, but not as a matter of principle. Once I was in the factory canteen and one of the English women said to me, 'Rampal, you finish my milk. I am not thirsty any more.' Of course she did not know that I would never do such a thing, and as I did not like to hurt her feelings I pretended that I did not care for milk. Yet I felt disgusted at the idea of finishing something that someone else had left. English people do not have this rule. I have not visited their homes much, but I have seen how they eat in public. Jamaicans are the same – I know because I have visited our Jamaican neighbour's house.

I do not understand why people differ so much in their customs. Tell me, do not all men inhabit the same world? Is not mankind one? Every man bleeds the same kind of blood; you will not find any race that bleeds water or milk. There is no human being who does not feel cold in winter and hot in summer, who does not feel hunger and thirst. We are all the

same, but why do we all have such different rules for living?
There is only one way of begetting children, but there are so
many different forms of marriage. There is only one way of
getting nourishment, but there are a hundred different ways of
sitting down to table. There is only one way of keeping warm,
but a hundred different fashions of dress.

English, Jamaicans, Indians, all have their different ways,
and each prefer their own. Indeed no one can say that one
people's ways are better than another's, how much good or
how much evil there is in each. For each man loves the laws
of the land where he was born.

Chapter 31

BRINGING UP CHILDREN

THREE of my children have lived much of their lives in
England, and the fourth was born here, so England will be the
home of their childhood. But we cannot help but bring them
up in the Indian way for we can only rear them in the manner
that is natural and familiar to us.

In some ways the way in which English people bring up
their children is good. They are rich, they have nothing to
worry about, they can give their children anything they want.
Does anyone in India have so much to spend on his children?
Or can the Indian government afford to give so much milk
away? Here every child sees the doctor regularly and his
mother, being educated, knows more about what sort of food
and clothing he should be given. Even we have been able to
give our little Pappi all kinds of things which we could never
have afforded to give the others, for they were born in India.

Yet English people seem to have little affection for their
children. Sons and daughters take themselves off the moment
they are grown, so what is the use of affection, or love? In

India we believe that if we give our children all the love that is in us and all the comforts we can afford, then when they are grown-up they will in turn provide for us without any prompting, and make the name of our family shine. They are our all, and we live for their sake. Let me tell you a story to show how it is in India.

In our village there was an old woman who had one son. That son died in his youth, leaving a wife and a little daughter. When she heard of her son's death that old woman shut herself inside her house and wept day and night for him. For weeks she neither ate nor drank, and her eyes grew dim with weeping. Losing her child was to her as if one of her limbs had been severed. She wanted to die yet she had to go on living. When we were little children we used to see her going about the village weeping and lamenting for her dead son. We used to laugh at her, because we did not understand, and say, 'Bebe is singing again.' Now what will English people say to that? Those to whom I told this story said that the old woman must be foolish to grieve for so long. But we do not think she was foolish.

Her grand-daughter also used to laugh at her when she was little, but as she grew up she came to understand that her grandmother was grieving. When at last the old woman died, this girl called to mind something that her grandmother had said. The old woman had once told her, 'My son always said that when I died he would shower silver coins on my bier as a sign of affection and sorrow.' The girl believed that her father must have put aside some money somewhere for this purpose and sure enough, when she searched the house she found a pot of coins hidden under the floor. At the funeral she scattered the coins on her grandmother's pyre on her father's behalf to mark the love that had been between mother and son. In India a mother's life is bound up with her child. English people do not understand this and would say that these villagers were sentimental and wasteful. But where is the need for sentiment in an English family? If anyone is sick or in need, the government will provide for him. Parents and children require nothing from each other. In India we look to our kin for help, here people look to the government.

English people are not strict with their children and do not beat them. In fact I was told that if you beat your child here, the police will come for you and take you to the courts. I have always believed that it is good to be a little strict with children. In India our elders say that 'a sickle will never cut the grass unless you sometimes strike it against a stone.' Children need to be 'sharpened' like this from time to time. If they cry we are distressed by their misery, but the pain that they feel is necessary and healthy. Bringing up children is a great responsibility. I often feel that but for my children my life would have no value. If they were all to go away there would be no reason for me to continue to live. I might as well die or leave the world to become an ascetic.

I should like my sons to study and become qualified men. In England they will have the chance to do this. I do not want them to be like me, obliged to labour and sweat because I have no education. I am anxious about Sarinder's schooling. His reports are quite good, but he does not study at all at home and he seems lazy to me. My father always used to tell me that the wise man always gets up early and goes to sleep early. He was always trying to impress this idea upon my elder brother, but he took no notice, and see what a failure he became. I tell my son this but he does not listen. His disobedience makes me fear that he is becoming like the English boys he mixes with at school – entirely without regard for his parents' commands. 'It does not matter if you do not get out of bed the minute you wake,' I tell him. 'You can sit up and read a book until you are ready.' But he does not take any notice; he watches television until late at night and cannot get up in time in the morning. His mother also has to get ready and go to her factory in the morning, so there is no one to stand over him and force him to be ready in time.

One day I was so worried about Sarinder's education that I determined to go and meet his teacher myself. I could not explain my doubts in English so I took an Indian acquaintance who could interpret for me. I told the head mistress that I feared that my son would lag behind in English and would be unable to get good qualifications when he grew older. She said that his English was fairly good but his main weakness was mathematics. Of course, I did not know enough English to judge Sarinder's knowledge of the language myself, so I did not doubt her word. I said to her that if she gave me a text-book I would try to coach him myself. But when I took the book home I could not understand it at all. Mathematics was my best subject when I was at school, but I could make neither head nor tail of this book. All the problems and methods were quite different from what I had learnt in my village school, so I had to return the book. 'Now my son is in the same position as I was when I was a boy,' I thought to myself. 'Just as my parents were unable to guide me in my education, so I am help-less to help my own son.'

Sometimes I curse this television and wonder why I even bought it. I say to myself that it would be a good thing if it broke down, because then my children might study in the evenings. But here everyone keeps a television – what would my children say if we did not also keep one? We have a problem here because children cannot help doing as they see others do. English people are in the majority here and so our children are bound to copy their ways. We cannot force them to conform to our ways. Now my children go to school; how can I tell what habits they are learning there or what they are being taught? If my daughters want to go to dances and meet English boys when they grow older, how will we be able to stop them? Suppose Asha were to get mixed up with a boy here, we could do nothing unless we were to rush her off to India and get her married immediately over there. In fact, if my wife were to come to me and say, 'Asha likes such-and-such a boy,' it would by then already be too late for me to do anything. In India, if a girl were to get involved with some boy there would be such a to-do that she would hardly dare tell her mother in the first place. So if my wife were to mention such a thing to me, I would know that things had gone too far already to be checked. I would be helpless. An Indian carpenter whom I know over here had a son who married an English girl and he was so furious that he turned them out of the house. He made a great fuss, beating his breast and asking why such a thing had to happen in his family. He did not even invite the couple home for the wedding of his other son. I would not do that kind of thing if one of my children wanted to marry an English person, because I realise that it would be useless. If they had become so English as to want to arrange their own marriages, then it would already be too late for me to object. I do not want them to be unhappy and so this is a serious problem for me. I cannot make my children do as I say; I can only explain to them what I think is right and just hope that they will follow those customs that I look upon as best.

Chapter 32

PEACE OF MIND AGAIN

IT is difficult to judge what will happen to us immigrant people in the future, or how long we shall be allowed to stay. But one thing is sure; even if English people do not send us home, we shall go home of our own accord as soon as there is no longer work for us to do here. Most of the Indians who come here are like me, village people in need of work, and they come here to earn money, not just for the fun of the trip. If any says he is here for a holiday, he is telling a lie. Would anyone work in another's house if he had plenty to eat in his own? Why else should we leave the country where we were born and where we have our land and kin? For myself, I can see our family staying here for another ten or fifteen years, until the children have finished their education and I have plenty of savings to take home with me.

Now that I have become used to this country, my family are

here with me and I have a good job, I do not altogether regret coming, in spite of all the difficulties I had to face at first. I only wish that I had been given a truer picture of England before I came. But I was misled, and ignorant of what I should really find here. Though I found money and comfort here which I could not earn in India, I also found loneliness and anxiety.

Now I have come through that time of trouble and have found peace of mind again. Each day passes quietly and in the same way. Every morning I get up early at about six o'clock. I get the baby's milk ready and then go to the park on my cycle. Each day I throw several pounds of grain to the pigeons there. (In India we always give food to poor people, or to cows or birds: one must give as well as receive.) When I come back I heat Pappi's milk and make tea for us all. After that, I light a stick of incense and burn it before all the gods and goddesses in our house. I turn over the names of all the saints and sages in my heart and pray to God, 'Father, true Lord, take thought for me also this day.' When I have done this I go to work, laugh and chat with the people there and work hard all day.

I seldom go for trips anywhere – in fact I have not been outside London more than a few times. Once I went to Bradford to meet the *hakim* I used to work with and another time I went to Peterborough to visit another Indian friend. Once we all went into the country to visit the parents of an English girl who is married to a friend of mine. We had to get out at a little station and walk for several miles to reach the house. When we came home at night the station was quite dark and silent, with just a few lanterns lighting the platform. I was reminded of the little village railway stations of the Punjab where just one or two trains call each day and I was surprised, for I had always had the impression that all English people lived in big bustling towns.

On Sundays I quite often attend the *gurudvara* and spend a few hours listening to the hymns which they sing there. Very occasionally we go to see an Indian picture (Indians hire big cinemas on Sundays and show their own Hindi films there). But we do not go very often – after all, we saw our fill of Hindi

pictures while we were in Delhi. Sometimes I watch the television in the evening to see the news; I got up early in the
morning the day the American astronauts landed on the moon
to watch the transmissions they sent. These are the only things
which interest me, and apart from these I have no leisure
activities, for I do not go to pubs and clubs as English men do.
I just occupy myself around the house and sit with my family.

I have not changed in my outward habits since coming here;
I eat, sleep and talk in the same way as I used to do in Delhi.
When I am at work I often sit cross-legged on my chair, just as
I used to do in India. Even if the manager comes in, I still go on
squatting like that. And I still find it easier to work sitting on
the floor with my tools spread out around me, rather than at a
table. But though I am the same man as I was in India, I have
come through many experiences before finding peace of mind.
I am grateful to God that now he has made me the most contented of men.

Part Three

SATYA'S STORY

*

Chapter 33

A PUNJABI FAMILY

OUR childhood was a royal time. How happily it passed. Do you know, it is more than twenty years since I left my parents' house; but I don't think I have ever been so happy as in those village days. I have been in England for about five years and before that I spent sixteen years in Delhi. I have seen something of life in that time.

I suppose we were not what English people would call rich, yet we never lacked for anything we wanted. We thought ourselves well off. My father kept a shop and also owned a little land. His father had emigrated to America long before I was born, leaving my grandmother behind. He never returned from America but for some time he kept sending his wife and son money. Then when he heard that my father had married and set up his own family and could support himself, he stopped sending money. But it meant that my father was well provided for until he could stand on his own two feet. Don't ask me what my grandfather did over there – if someone asked my parents, 'What are Rampal and Satya doing in England?' do you think they would be able to tell all the details of our life here? They would only be able to say, 'Well, we know that they have bought their own house and that they are earning good money,' and that would be all. If my grandfather had ever come back we should no doubt have heard all about what he did in America, what life was like over there at that time, how he lived and how the world ticks in America. We might have learnt something about the ways of the West. But he never did come back. We never knew how he died. He was illiterate himself and he used to get a man he knew to write letters to us on his behalf. When he died that man wrote to inform us of his death and there the matter ended. But I do know that he married some *Mem* over there and had some sons and daughters by her.

My mother's father also emigrated. He went to Canada. Yes, even at that time quite a few men were emigrating from our district, though in those days it was usually only the men who went and not the wives and children. He also used to send money home to his family so my mother also came from a household which was well provided for. He came home once on a visit, before I was born, and built a fine house in his village with the money he had earned over there. It was a beautiful house with five big balconies, much bigger than the house we live in here. My mother used to say that, if only she had had a brother, he might be living in that house now, making use of it properly and carrying on my grandfather's name. As it is, I don't think it is even rented to anyone at present.

I never actually saw my mother's father in the flesh, but we used to have a photo of him in our house and I remember looking at it when I was little – a big Sikh with a beard and turban. When my grandfather went to Canada he left his wife and daughter in the care of his younger brother, but he kept on sending them money. He loved my mother very much because she was his only child. He used to write to her, 'Don't worry about anything. I will do everything for your daughters. When I come back I myself will see that they are married well and give them good dowries.' But he died before he could keep his promise.

When he died my mother inherited the whole of his land intact because she had no brothers. They were a farming family and had quite a lot of land. My father was also the only surviving child of his parents and so he too inherited his father's property intact. His father's land was only a little, not as much as my mother's land. The land my mother inherited is rented out to tenants – they give half the produce to us and keep half for themselves. But my father farmed his own land himself in addition to looking after his shop. He never rented it out or even employed labourers. I say he worked his land himself, but with the income from the shop and from my mother's land he was never in such a position that he had to break his bones or kill himself with hard work in the fields.

So you can see why we considered ourselves comfortably off. In my parents' house, we children never felt any need, never worried about anything. What we ate, we ate; what was spilt was spilt; what was left was thrown away. We children did not know our own wealth, we were hardly aware of 'ours' and 'theirs'. It is only when you get married that you have to start worrying for yourself about money. It is a good thing I did not know beforehand how many worries and responsibilities you have to take up when you get married or I might never have taken a husband. It is only then that you have to start thinking, 'Better set by half of this food for to-morrow, better save half of what I have bought for another day.' Look at my children, now. None of them ever has any worry about himself. It is I who thinks, 'Suppose they fall ill,' or, 'I must remember to do this that or the other for them.' In the same way, when I was a child my parents never let us worry about anything. We got up happy in the morning and went to bed happy at night.

Chapter 34

SATYA'S VILLAGE

OUR village is quite big and its population is still increasing. Some villages in our Punjab are even bigger – for instance my husband's village. That has some ten thousand people living in it. It is so large that weddings go on without you knowing anything about them until you hear the band playing. In a small place everybody knows everybody else's business and they know who is marrying whom well in advance. Our village is divided into four *mohallas* with about four hundred people in each, but even then we did not know every single person in the village well, only those in our own *mohalla*. It was within our own *mohalla* that we would give and get invitations, there would be comings and goings from one house to another. The rest of the village we did not know so intimately. We just knew that they were there, that was all. My father knew them all though, and they knew him, because he was quite a big man in the village.

Our house was quite large, with five big rooms. At first it was *kaccha*, but later on my parents used the money my grandfather had sent from Canada to make some improvements. It had a walled courtyard where there were some trees growing, and under the trees they made a paved area and installed a pump. They faced the walls too; before that I remember us having to replaster the walls with mud every now and then. Behind the house there was a stable for the buffaloes – we kept two buffaloes – and a place to tie them up. In those days there was no electricity and we had to burn oil lamps in the house. Nowadays they have turned the little villages into towns – in every house a radio playing, in every street electricity. But then there was no electricity. All the farm work was done with bullocks. In my childhood, when they gathered in the wheat they would collect all the sheaves in one place as they cut them and then set the bullocks to work threshing them. Under their feet the ears would split and the grain separate from the chaff, which was used as fodder. They might spend a whole month doing that work. Nowadays, there is a machine to do it and the job is tied up in one hour flat. Even when I was little, the village land was watered by an irrigation canal so there was no longer any need to keep bullocks to work the Persian wells. And now there are tube wells also, worked by electricity. And as for ploughing, don't they have tractors these days? Even if every man can't afford to buy one, if there is just one in the village he can rent it from the owner. So these days you no longer find that every family keeps bullocks, only some of them.

In our village there were people of all castes – Brahmans,

Khatris, barbers, carpenters, tanners, cobblers – but mainly Jats. Our village lives mainly by farming. It is good fertile soil there. The thing is nowadays, even if the soil is poor, the government gives the farmers fertiliser and where you got four sacks of wheat before, now you get eight. The government has really set progress going. But even when I was a child the living in our village was good. The only thing we could not grow was rice. Rice did not grow at all well there – you have to go a bit farther to find good rice-growing soil. Otherwise we grew wheat, maize, lentils, *ber* and mangoes. One or two people in the village kept mango orchards. And ground nuts grew very well there. My father still grows and sells them. We used to eat the nuts freshly roasted. First you dig them out of the soil like potatoes and then you dry them and roast them on a wood fire. We used to roast maize cobs from our own fields too. I remember how delicious they used to taste.

Our village is a fine place. If it is God's will that we should ever go back to India I will take you there and show you. You will see yourself what a happy place it is.

Chapter 35

DADI

In India childhood is a time of affection. We were a big family – five girls and two boys – though my younger brother was only born after I had already got married – but we were always surrounded by such love and tenderness. I think it was our grandmother who loved us the best. She loved us especially because having only the one son she had no other little grand-children to cherish. In fact she had had other children besides my father, but all her babies used to die. She had four girls and one boy, but as soon as ever they were born they would fall ill and die, one after the other. So one day, before my father was born, she prayed to Baba Nanak, the Sikh Guru. She said, 'Baba Nanak, if only you give me one son and he survives, I will make a Sikh of him in memory of your kindness.' So when my father was born she kept her vow to Guru Nanak and never allowed his hair to be cut. (That is why he is a Sikh and always wears a beard and turban, otherwise his side of the family were all Hindus.) In fact I can remember once when my father was very sick and the doctor advised that he should shave his head for the sake of his health. This happened before my eyes and I can remember it clearly because I was quite a big girl at the time. So my grandmother said, 'I know he is ill, but if you cut his hair my vow will be broken and then he is quite certain to die. If you must cut his hair, shave just a little off one side, that might have some effect.' Well, my father was laid up in bed for six months but Dadi would not let him have his head shaved, she was so afraid of losing him. She was sure that he would come to some harm if her vow were not kept. She loved him dearly, and that is why she loved us especially too. My mother used to spank us if we were naughty, but Dadi would always try to stop her. She would be angry if our mother laid a hand on us. 'Why are you beating the little ones?' she would say. And we loved her even more than our own mother. It was her we would run to if we wanted anything rather than to our mother, her skirts we would cling to. The day our Dadi died, it was as though a great hunger had come into our lives.

Chapter 36

MISCHIEF AND PUNISHMENT

I HAVE one elder sister and one elder brother, the rest are younger than myself. How can I say which one I love the most? The only difference among brothers and sisters is that you play more with those who are younger than yourself and get hidings from those who are older. Mind you, we girls used to squabble a good deal among ourselves. We used to tease my little sister, Gita – the one who is now married to my husband's brother – by sitting her on a big wooden peg which used to stick out of the wall, and making her cry to be taken down.

We were often getting into mischief. I'll tell you what happened one day. I had a friend called Dipu. We were fond of playing with our dolls together. If anyone in her family discarded any old torn garment she would bring it along and we would share it between us to make dolls' dresses, and I would do the same for her. One day one of the village women washed a new skirt and spread it out in the sun to dry. She was a new bride and it was part of her trousseau, beautiful peach-coloured cloth it was made from, not dull-coloured coarse cotton like village people wear ordinarily. And there must have been yards and yards of cloth in it – women wore big wide skirts in those days. Anyway, Dipu made off with it, and the pair of us sat down and divided it between us, sitting hidden in the cowshed among the bags of chaff. When they discovered that the skirt had vanished our neighbours made a great fuss. 'Who has taken our daughter-in-law's skirt? Who has stolen it?' They were afraid someone had taken it for the purpose of witchcraft. Village people in India know how to perform witchcraft and usually they use some piece of their victim's clothing to carry it out. And a recently married woman is especially susceptible. For days they kept up the hue and cry, abusing everyone and swearing and cursing, but they never suspected us children. One day some time after this an old man in the village died and we went to attend his funeral feast. We were rather greedy and Dipu said to me, 'I fancy another help ing.' 'Wipe your hands first,' I said to her, 'or they will see that they are sticky and know that you have already had a share.' In her pocket she had a piece of that very cloth, the skirt she had stolen, and she took it out to wipe her hands – who knows about handkerchiefs in the villages? We had thought that the matter of the skirt had been finished and forgotten, but some-one recognised the cloth and remarked, 'That is funny, Dipu's rag just matches that skirt of our sister-in-law's, the one that was stolen.' When I heard this I knew that there would be trouble and as soon as I could I returned all the bits of cloth that were with me to Dipu. I was afraid that my brother would find out – he always liked a chance to give us girls a hiding, it was a very bad habit of his. Sure enough, that night those people came to Dipu's house and demanded to know what she had done with the skirt. There was a furious quarrel between the two families. 'We are not going until we have got back every inch of that cloth. What did your daughter tear it up for?' they said. By the time Dipu had found all the bits the whole courtyard seemed full of peach coloured stuff – some we had made into doll's clothes, little skirts, *saris*, shirts, pyjamas, and some into doll's bedding. When I saw what trouble she had got into I said to her, 'I am not friends with you any more. From now on I am not playing with you, it is too much of a risk, thank you very much.' But what do little children know of right or wrong? Our thoughts never went farther than our dolls and their clothes. If anyone had a new suit the only interest it had for us was, 'How soon will it become old and worn enough for them to let us tear it up for doll's clothes?'

Chapter 37

'I NEVER WENT TO SCHOOL'

As for school – we girls never saw the inside of a school in our lives. My big brother used to go to school in a town some miles from our village. Every day he used to go on foot along the sandy, dusty road. My little brother, the one who was born after I got married, must have gone to school too. If there had at least been a school in our own village no doubt we sisters would have studied as well (in those days there were no schools in the villages as there are nowadays). But people were unwilling to send their daughters to the town to study. Our parents would say that the boys might tease us, or we might get into mischief on the way. In those days young girls did not go out a lot.

I often think how if only I had been born in some big town I might have got the chance to be educated, as I regret sorely not having been to school. But there it was – it was my fate to be born in a village. When I look at my children I think of all the opportunities they have and hope that they will study a lot. Then they will come to something in life, things will go well for them. Because an illiterate person like myself is always dependent on other people. If you cannot read or write, your business always proceeds slowly because you have to wait on the will of others. 'Let some educated person come along,' you say, 'and I will get him to help me to write this letter, or read this note, I will ask him how to get this thing done.' A person who is literate – he wants something done so he gets up and does it for himself that very minute. An illiterate person is as helpless as an invalid. If a bed-ridden old man wants a fresh cup of tea he has to wait for someone to come along and fill the kettle and turn on the gas. If he were only capable of doing it himself, do you think he would put up with the cold tea in the pot?

Later on, when I was in Delhi, I picked up a little *Gurmukhi*, and recently I have started to learn some English. I just picked up *Gurmukhi* here and there, looking at shop signs, books, anything. Slowly, slowly, you come to learn the letters. If there is a story in Punjabi I can follow it if I read carefully. If you read a story over and over again you come to know what it is all about. I used to read religious books mostly in Punjabi. Look, I have just got a new one from an Indian shop. I like to read a bit whenever I have time. Even now, if I compare *Gurmukhi* with other scripts I find that I like it the best of all. I find it easy to learn and when I read it, I understand what the words mean. If I read English I lose track of what is written because I don't know all the words. If I had been to school as a child it might be easier for me to learn a new language now. A person gets into the habit of studying.

Of course it is quite different for the girls of to-day. Now, if you please, village girls not only go to school, their mothers give them bicycles to take them there. Just before coming to England I saw girls in our village, twenty or twenty-five at a time, get together to go to school on their bicycles each morning. In the evening they would all go off in a bunch to meet the girls of the next village. To-day there is much more liberty for girls, all yesterday's customs seem to have changed.

Chapter 38

LEARNING

IN India little girls have to learn how to do all the housework at quite an early age. At first, when we were tiny, we were not expected to do any work but even then we learnt through playing. We would smooth out a place in the roadway or in an alley – hardly any buses or cars ever came along village streets in those says – and then make little houses out of mud. Then we would make a doll out of rags. 'This is the daughter-in-law of the house,' we would say. Of course dolls can't talk, but we would make up her conversations for her. 'She says, "Water the buffaloes"; she says she is hungry and it's time for dinner.' So we would mix the dust with water, knead the clay we had made and roll it out into little *chapatties*, copying what we had seen our mothers do. Or sometimes the bigger girls would teach us how to make dolls' clothes out of scraps of cloth so that quite early on we got used to the feel of a needle in our hands. Gradually through playing at keeping house we would get practice for the real thing.

Once we were about seven or eight our mother expected us to give a hand in earnest, although as there were five of us girls, the tasks were never too heavy. If the pots and pans had to be scoured, then the five of us would set to work and the job would soon get done. Our mother would explain to us how everything should be done and allocate tasks to each of us – someone would have to fold the bedding, someone fetch the water, a third would wash the dishes. With the work distributed like that it was never too burdensome. From time to time we would re-plaster the floors of our house; we would all set to, fetching the water and mixing it with the mud and cow-dung to make a good paste. Then our mother would show us how to spread it in each room and make it nice and smooth.

Even when we were supposed to be working we would turn the work into play. We would be sent in pairs to fetch water, each with a pot on her head, but often on the way back we would take it into our heads to use some of the water to mix with clay and make miniature water pots, just like those the potter's wife used to come round selling. Or sometimes we would go to the well to wash the clothes there, wetting them and then beating them on the stones until they were clean. We had no sense of time at all – what did we know of clocks and watches who had hardly seen one in all our lives? We would just keep an eye on the sun. As long as it was shining we would say, 'Come on, let's stay a little longer and play.' Only when the sun went down and the air began to get cool did we know it was time to set off for home. Or we would watch out for the boys coming home from school and judge the time by their return. Nothing sticks in a child's mind, and if we were enjoying ourselves we would forget what errand we had been sent for.

If we had to take the buffaloes to the pond to water them, that was the greatest fun. We would have to drag the buffaloes there but once they got to the pond they would plunge into the water and sit down in it. Then we would have a difficult job to get them out again.

It used to be my special task to bring in the cattle at night if it started to rain. As soon as I heard the wind starting up I would run to untie the buffaloes and the cow from where they were tethered, and take them into the shed. One night I remember, I had untied the cow and her calf – it was a big strong calf – but when I took them indoors to tie them up again, the calf started to tug at the rope. I had the other end of the rope in my hand but I did not have the presence of mind to grip it hard and instead of me pulling the calf inside, it began to drag me outside. It started to run off down the path, the calf in front and me bumping along behind. I thought I was done for but I did not let go. I remember how scared I was. Then it occurred to me that a little way down the path there was a pond and cows don't like to go through water as a buffalo will.

Sure enough, when it got there the calf halted and turned about, and I managed to pick myself up. I regained my breath and led the calf off home, but how bruised and battered I was! In fact I was always getting into scrapes and having accidents.

Another time – I could hardly have been more than four at the time – I was sent to get some hay from the top of a pile of bales of fodder stacked in a shed. But the bales were stacked very loosely and when I tried to scramble to reach the top I slipped and fell to the floor, hurting myself really badly. Nobody found out what had happened to me until an old lady chanced to hear me crying and picked me up. I had broken a bone in my foot and for five days I was fainting with pain much of the time. There was no doctor in the village – what village had a doctor in those days? But one of the villagers was experienced in traditional remedies and he used to come to our house every day to bind up my foot.

Chapter 39

TEMPLES AND FEASTS

WE did not have many outings when we were small; we knew every twist and turn of the paths of our own village but seldom ventured outside it. Where was there to go, anyway? There are no *bazars* in the countryside. And if we went anywhere it had to be on foot as there were few buses in those days. I have often noticed that the town children in India are seldom as tough as the village children. They are weak in their bodies and have no stamina. For in the towns, whenever people go out they say 'Might as well take a *tonga*' or 'Why not take a bus?' When I was a girl village people knew that if they wanted to get anywhere they would have to walk there. In that way they become tough right from their childhood.

One of our amusements however was to go to the temple or the *gurudvara* with our mothers. In India there is no ban on Hindus and Sikhs going to each other's temples, although very strict Sikhs do not visit Hindu temples, so we went to both the *gurudvara* in our own village and the Hindu temples in the villages nearby. My mother was a very pious woman. People of her generation had genuine faith and devotion to God, they worshipped sincerely. Nowadays people regard God as a sort of lottery – you make your prayer and if you are lucky you get what you want; if you are unlucky you go without.

We used to go with our mother to the temple of the goddess Sitala in a neighbouring village. We would prepare sweet cakes and offer them with a rupee each. We little ones would watch the ceremonies going on there with great curiosity. And then when we got home my mother would invite five or six unmarried girls to our house. She would wash their feet and give them some of the cakes to eat (In India people honour girls in this way, as representing the goddess). Our mother used to worship the goddess Devi a lot – even now I keep a picture of her on my wall; there she is, riding on her tiger.

The festivals that came round each year were great fun too. There was the day of Hoi Mata, another goddess. They used to tell a story about it, how once there was a woman whose children all died in infancy. She did not cremate their poor little bodies or bury them but put them in a basket in her kitchen so that she could remember them. When her last little son was born someone told her she should keep a fast in honour of Hoi Mata so that the goddess would protect the child. Well, she did keep the fast and when she was about to finish her fasting in the evening, her little boy came into the kitchen and started to beg for a taste of the sweetmeats she was preparing. Then suddenly all the other little children came to life and started crying for sweets too. The woman was rewarded for her devotion. People over here might laugh at a story like that. They would say, 'Go on, how could dead children come to life again all of a sudden? Was she a doctor or something?' But the women would retell these stories each year when the festivals came round and we liked to listen to them. On the feast of Krishna Janam Ashtami an old Brahman woman used to come round to each house and recount the story of the god Krishna's birth, how his parents were imprisoned by his wicked uncle, how he was born in the jail, how the doors of the jail miraculously flew open to set them free. The other women would ask her how they ought to keep the fast, what things they were allowed to eat and what things they should not eat. She would tell them everything, what rituals they should perform and what was the correct food to prepare in the evening. At night she would come again and authorise them to break the fast. She would touch the sweets which they had prepared, so as to consecrate them, and then the sweets would be shared out. The village women would give her grain or money in payment. She was a poor widow with several children to bring up and that was the way she scratched a living for herself. We children were too young to keep the fast ourselves but we made sure we got a share of the sweets all the same. We were not going to miss a chance of good things to eat and thought it great fun, even though we did not understand the religious reasons behind it.

Chapter 40

ELDERS AND DAUGHTERS

BUT whenever we went out of the village, whether to the temple or anywhere else, it was always with one of our elders accompanying us. We were not allowed to go alone. In the villages fairs are often held on religious holidays and sometimes people wander about drunk at night and start fights. Our parents would not let us go if they thought there would be any such rough goings on. But if they were satisfied that it was not that sort of occasion they would agree to take us. They would never refuse any reasonable request because they did not like us to be left yearning for something if it was something they could let us have. They did not want us to accuse them, 'You never take us anywhere.' 'All right then, come along children, we will take you to the fair,' they would say. Then at the festival of Dussehra there would be dramatic performances at night; someone would be dressed up as the brave hero Rama, another as his wife Sita, others as gods and goddesses. They would act out all the old stories. Suppose I took my children back to the village now – I don't suppose those amusements would mean anything to them. They are just used to the television. And the television would mean nothing to village children.

Wherever we went as children it was never without asking our parents' permission. It did not matter whether we asked our mother or our father or our Dadi, but our elders must give us permission before we ventured out. In India parents have much more control over their children than they do here. When we were very small we could wander about fairly freely, but once we girls passed into our teens, our mother would say, 'Now then, no going off to play outside, why can't you sit down and do some sewing?' She used to teach us how to cut out and sew our own clothes, how to crochet and do embroidery. At that age, parents start to keep a closer watch on their daughters. In the towns they are even stricter. Do you know what I have seen them do in Delhi? People of good families employ older women as chaperones. Sometimes all the parents who live in one block of flats club together to pay such a woman to take their daughters to school in the *tonga*. At break time, if the girls get hungry, they tell their chaperone and she will go out and buy them something to eat. Then she will bring the girls back home in the afternoon. And in the school holidays, if the parents want to send their daughters to take a vacation course in needlework, the same chaperone takes them there too. While the girls are inside learning, all the chaperones get together for a good gossip.

They don't do that in the villages. But all the same we would always be accompanied by an adult if we went out. In the evening our mother would take us out to the fields to go to the toilet or we would go for a little stroll with her, but only if she was ready to take us. She always used to say, 'If you have no business outside the house, then just sit at home peacefully and do some sewing. Or if you have nothing better to do, then pull your *charpoy* into the courtyard and take some sleep. What is the use of roaming around outside? If you stay at home then no one can point their fingers at you and say, "So-and-so's daughter was wandering about to-day in such-and-such a place." Sit at home, keep yourself to yourself, and no one can gossip. Dogs won't yap if no one goes near them.' I must have caught my mother's habit because even now I don't enjoy visiting very much. If you stay at home you can relax in your oldest clothes and nobody will mind. Some women enjoy going around and poking their noses into other people's business, but I still follow my mother's advice. After all, if people want to see me, they know where to find me.

My father was very strict with us also in that respect. We knew that if we wandered out without his permission he would be waiting for us with a good punishment in store. He was not often angry, but we had great respect for him and one glance from his eyes was enough to keep us in order. After all he was a Sikh, wasn't he? You must remember that he could look very intimidating with his big beard and turban.

As I grew older I came to understand why our parents kept such a close watch over us and to trust their judgement. For example, I remember on one occasion we had gone to bathe in the river Ganges at Haridwar. There is a fair there every year, but every twelfth year there is a special fair, much bigger than the annual gathering. It is called Kumb Mela, and huge crowds gather by the river at that time. People throw coins and even pieces of gold into the river and give money away as charity. Well, we arrived at the inn and settled down to sleep, but at about two o'clock in the morning we were woken by our father. 'Come, children,' he said, 'We will go and bathe now, not in the morning.' I thought to myself, 'Pitaji must be out of his senses to wake us up at such an unearthly hour. How silly to go now when we might be sleeping peacefully.' But we went down to the river and bathed in the sacred water. There was not a soul around, not a trace of a crowd – people are not in the habit of bathing at two in the morning, after all. We must have spent about an hour there by the river and then we came back and made ourselves a cup of tea. But even as we were coming back the rush started. You never saw such a stampede. At the Kumb Mela enormous crowds gather and whoever stumbles on the way to the river will never be able to pick himself up, let alone get near the water. People trample over one another to get there. We heard the loudspeaker they were using to try to control the crowds, and every now and then there would be announcements that such-and-such a number of people had already been crushed to death or injured in the rush. Some of the women who had stayed behind while their husbands went to bathe started weeping; they were afraid they would never see them again. So I said to my father, 'What a good thing that we went so early.' 'Yes,' he said, 'I have been to Haridwar four times in my life already, my dear. I knew just how it would be.' So I realised that his judgement had been sensible, even though I had thought he was crazy at the time.

Chapter 41

PREPARING FOR MARRIAGE

W HEN I was fifteen my parents felt that it was time to start thinking about my marriage. Some relatives of ours were acquainted with my husband's[1] family and when they suggested

1. Satya seldom refers to, or addresses her husband by his name. In India it is considered disrespectful for a wife to use her husband's personal name, and some circumlocution is used instead. Indeed it is considered impolite to address anyone who is one's elder, or to whom respect is due, by their personal name.

the match my parents felt that it would be a highly satisfactory one. And as my parents-in-law were also looking for a bride for their youngest son, they thought nothing could be better than to promise Gita to him. So the two of us were engaged. The fact that my husband's household are Hindus whilst my father is a Sikh did not matter. In our part of India, Sikhs and Hindus do intermarry sometimes: caste is a stronger consideration than religion. In our district people won't marry their daughters to boys of the same religion if they are of different castes. Well, my father is a Khatri by caste and my husband is a Khatri also, and therefore the difference of religion was not considered important. And the match was a good one from all other points of view as my husband had good employment and had the reputation of being a steady character.

In this country marriage is just a hasty affair and no wonder the boy and girl often leave each other soon after. In India it is a much more weighty matter. So many relatives are involved, so many detailed arrangements. Even the engagement itself is a matter of ceremony. My father had to make so many gifts to my husband's family before the match was concluded. And after that my husband and I remained engaged for three whole years. We did not see each other during that time of course – he stayed in his own house and I stayed in mine. Even during an engagement the match can be broken if anything goes wrong – even after all that gift-making it is only a kind of trial arrangement. So my father continued to make inquiries whenever he could from people acquainted with my husband's family, so as to confirm in his own mind that his choice had been a good one.

Did I worry whether I should like the husband my parents had picked for me? Of course I didn't. Why should I have had any doubts? Look, if I say to you, 'Go fetch such-and-such a thing from the shops,' it is you that the worry will fall upon, isn't it? If I have trusted you in the first place so far as to ask you to get a thing on my behalf, I shan't fret that maybe I won't like what you have chosen for me. But you may think, 'Suppose Satya says it is not good enough, then I shall feel ashamed.' So I trusted my parents that they would choose someone good for me. I thought, 'My parents know my habits, so they know what sort of place I would be happy in.' I knew that they would have considered carefully before committing me to a particular household whether I was likely to be happy or miserable there. At the most I used to think, 'Even if I don't fancy my husband, never mind. I can always run back home and live with my parents the rest of my life.' I looked at it this way; if I had picked a boy myself and our marriage had not worked well, I could never have expected my parents to take my side and give me much sympathy. They could then say, 'We told you so, it serves you right.' But if the choice was theirs in the first place they could hardly blame me if things didn't turn out well. That was how I reasoned to myself. So you see I was not at all troubled by the idea of marrying someone I had never seen before.

To tell you the truth, I thought more about what sort of mother-in-law I should get than about the husband chosen for me. If your mother-in-law is a gentle sort, the kind of person who gets on well with everyone, then you have nothing to worry about. But if she is a quarrelsome old thing then your marriage can hardly be happy. I have seen some mothers-in-law who work their daughters-in-law like slaves and only get up from their beds themselves when someone says, 'Let's all have a glass of milk now.' For in India it is usual for a mother-in-law and daughter-in-law to live together. Nowadays there are some who do not share a house but generally speaking the young couple will sleep in one room and the husband's parents in the next room. As it turned out I was to spend very little time with my mother-in-law as my husband worked in Delhi and she lived in the village, but even in such circumstances as those, a bride is expected to change her ways to suit those of her husband's house and not impose her own will.

That was the main thing which my mother was anxious to

teach me in preparation for my marriage. 'When you go to your husband's house,' she used to say, 'Don't you offer your own opinion about anything at first. Just keep quiet and listen to the others. If anyone asks you your opinion just say that you agree with them. When you are in your husband's house don't make the mistake of thinking that you are still at home with us. Here you can say, "I don't fancy that dish," or "I can't eat that," but over there don't make a fuss. Just take what is given you whether you like it or not.'

That was the advice I received from everyone before I got married and I think it is good sense. After all, if I go to visit a home where they all like to eat spinach every day and I order them to eat lentils just because I happen to prefer lentils they will feel, 'Who is she to tell us how to run our house?' I must try to fit in with their habits and I think it is because most people do this that our arranged marriages are usually successful.

Chapter 42

A VILLAGE WEDDING

You must remember that I was not married yesterday; my wedding took place some twenty years ago and was performed according to the customs of those days. For one thing, not all girls are married as young as I was. I was eighteen when my wedding took place and my sister was fourteen or fifteen. These days girls study and do courses in colleges and they are often twenty-one or even older when they come to get married. And modern weddings are often hurried affairs compared to the way our wedding was conducted, for my marriage took three whole days to complete.

My father went to great expense to get us girls married, and the preparations for our wedding began some time in advance.

'Don't ever let us give your in-laws cause to say that we did not treat them well,' my father used to say. There was a great busy-ness and bustle in the house for days beforehand. All the sweets for the wedding were made at home from the best milk and sugar. Only the best home-made sweets would do in those days; now people just run across the road to the shop and order them from there. But even if we had wanted to do that, in a country village like ours there was no *bazar* where we could have bought such things ready made.

When my husband arrived in our village with his party it was very exciting, although as the bride I did not have much part to play in the proceedings. I just had to sit to one side whilst everything went on around me. My father went out to welcome them and all the members of the village *panchayat* were there too. They had prepared a place beforehand where the wedding party could be accommodated for the three days they were to stay in our village, where they could put their bedding and sleep at nights. Then they were regaled with a really fine meal – three or four different vegetable dishes as well as rice-pudding and fried pancakes. In the morning someone was sent to find out how many members of the party would like to drink milk, how many would prefer tea or butter milk. And my father gave each person whatever he asked for. Before each meal they were given as many sweets as they chose to tuck into before the main dishes were served.

So it went on for the whole three days which it took to complete the wedding ceremonies. My father never stinted anything. The groom's party were even given food in baskets when they went away in case they should feel hungry on the way. In those days people really knew how to entertain.

Of course my father had also provided a generous dowry for both my sister and myself. In India parents take great thought for their children's future. Long before a girl is old enough to get married her mother starts putting things aside for her dowry. English people just leave their sons and daughters to fend for themselves when they are grown, but amongst our Indian people I have never seen any parent fail to get their daughter married and to give her whatever they can for a dowry, however poor they may be. Even if they cannot do much they will do whatever is within their means. For some years my mother and father had been preparing my dowry, putting aside sometimes cloth for a *kamiz*, sometimes cloth for a shirt, sometimes money for the jewellery. Cloth was cheaper then than it is now and so the greater part of my dowry consisted of clothes for me, my husband and my in-laws. They were really beautiful clothes. There was jewellery also, all made of gold of course, and a ring for my husband. These days people give radios, cycles, sofa sets and all kinds of other things, but in those days these things were not available in the villages. Amongst our people everything is done with a lot of giving and receiving. Take my parents; at my marriage they had to give me and my in-laws so many things. They did the same for all my other sisters too. And when my children or my sisters' children get married, then also they will have to contribute something. After all, one of the first things the groom's parents will say when the match is first proposed is: 'All right, you are ready to give us your daughter, but what else will you give besides?' Again, when I was married, the handing over of the dowry was not the end of the matter. Each time I came home to visit my parents after the wedding I would take back some presents for my husband and in-laws when I returned. On my wedding day my father said, 'To-day we are giving you our daughters, but we shall send more gifts after them. This is not the end of the giving.'

Now that I have been long married myself I can see that this custom is good. The parents do all this out of their love for their daughter but there is also practical sense in it. From what I have seen with my own eyes I know that if a girl's parents are mean or don't keep sending things then it is the subject of daily wrangling in her in-laws' house. Her mother-in-law will pick on her and say, 'Your father didn't give us this, that or the other,' or 'What kind of pauper's house do you come from?' or, 'These clothes are not much good, couldn't your people do better than that?' And that is where the quarrelling begins. If the girl uses her senses she will be able to establish herself in her new household well enough, but all this makes it the harder for her because it reflects on her parents. And the bigger the marriage party her husband took with him to her wedding, the greater the number of people to whom her father's lack of means will have been evident. Fortunately I never had to suffer that kind of trouble because my father took great pains to give everything that could possibly be expected, but I have seen the sort of misery that can befall a girl if the greed of her in-laws is not satisfied.

In India, when a girl gets married, she usually only stays a little time in her husband's house at first. She will come back a few days after the wedding and remain with her parents for some time. If her parents-in-law need her services, if someone is ill for example, they may ask for her to be sent back very quickly but otherwise she will stay for a year or two in her parents' house before going to her husband's place again. When she goes for the second time she will stay a little longer – perhaps a month or two – with her husband. Only when she goes to him for the third time is it final. After all, if the parents rushed their daughter off to her husband's house as soon as they could after the wedding and didn't make sure that she spent quite a lot of time with them in the first years of her marriage, people would say to the girl, 'Dear, dear, what is the matter with your family? They can't love you very much as they never call you home to their house.' Isn't that what would come to their minds?

My case was a little different because my husband's elder brother's wife had recently died, leaving small children behind her, and I was needed to help take care of them. I was obliged to spend less time with my parents. My sister and I spent one night at our in-laws' house in their village and then came back home, but after a few months I went to join my husband in Delhi where he was working. On the first visit I only spent a couple of months with him, but after a few more months at home, I went back to Delhi for good. After all someone had to see the children off to school and cook food for my husband

and his brother. I was forced by circumstances, wasn't I? My
sister stayed at home rather longer; her husband was working
in Bikaner at that time and anyway she was too young to go
and live with him straight away.

I remember the first time Gita and I departed for our in-
laws' house, on the last day of the wedding. They sat us in a
tonga, and we both cried like anything. Indeed a bride who does
not cry when the time comes to leave her father's house will be
considered a very unloving daughter. How we wept! But
actually in our hearts we did not feel so sad as we sounded,
because after all we were not going alone. We were two sisters
and we had each other to keep ourselves company. And we
knew very well that we would be coming home again the next
day, so we were not really too distressed.

Yet when we arrived we felt too shy to speak. We didn't
know where to put ourselves, we felt so timid amongst all those
strangers. If someone said, 'Sit here,' we just sat there. If they
said, 'Do this,' we just did it, without saying anything. I felt
too shy even to ask where anything was or where I might go
to the toilet. In fact I always got on well with my mother-in-
law – she was a simple person and not at all quarrelsome – but
it is certainly true that my shyness gradually wore off. Each
time I visited my husband I felt less timid as I got into the
habit of being with him. Yet the first time I had been with him
alone I had just sat down consumed with shyness.

Our customs make it easy for the bride and groom to get to
know each other, even though they are strangers at first.
Their affection is given time to grow and they almost always
come to love each other. (That is how it was for my husband
and myself at least.)

When the bride first goes to her husband's house, she is not
made to do any work at all. They say to her, 'No need for you
to do any sweeping, no need for you to do any work in the
fields or go to the well.' The girl just sits down quietly and
they send her food when the meal is prepared. The first couple
of times I visited my husband I didn't have to do a thing, so of
course it seemed like a holiday for me. That way, it makes it

easier to like being in your husband's home. And then, during the first year of my marriage I was not with my husband very much but spent more time at my parents' house. Through seeing him for only a short while at a time, I would come to miss him when I wasn't with him. Because we met only occasionally our love had a chance to grow more strongly.

I have been fortunate in my marriage and I was pleased with the choice my father made for me. Love marriages are all very well – you may avoid the expense of dowries and all that kind of thing. But I have seen how often they break up afterwards. I never have any fears that I might be abandoned by my husband, and nor does he ever fear that I might leave him. We do not show affection by kissing in the street like people do here, but Indian marriages are not flimsy affairs. The ties which bind us together are firm and deep.

Chapter 43

LIVING IN THE CITY

WHEN I first came to Delhi we lived in a room at Pahar Ganj. At first I used to feel very depressed and lonely. I had no one of my own in Delhi other than my husband; in fact he was on his own too, for neither did he have any relatives there. Suddenly I had been snatched from the midst of my brothers and sisters to sit all alone in the big city, more than a hundred miles from my own village. At first I used to think, 'I am so far from my family, why did I ever come here?' But I think most women in India feel this way when they are first married. Once you have established your household you make friends in your new home, your babies start to come and then you begin to feel real affection for the place.

Soon after coming to Delhi I persuaded my elder brother to move there from the village also, and shortly he came to join us. Fortunately he found work quite easily and so his wife and children were able to follow him within a little while. In fact they shared our home for a time while we were living in Pahar Ganj before moving to quarters of their own at Karol Bagh. Once my brother had joined us I ceased to feel so cut off from my family.

Next my younger sister arrived – the one who is married to my husband's younger brother. They had previously been living in Bikaner in Rajasthan where he had been employed, but then he found work as a driver for some big industrial firm in Delhi. By that time we had moved to first floor quarters at Motiya Khan and they shared that flat with us for several years. We got on very well together, my sister and I. We used to share all our household expenses and had a joint budget while we were living together. We even discovered another relative of ours in Delhi at that time – a cousin of my father's who lived near the Ajmeri Gate. So soon we felt that we had re-assembled our family around us and I began to regard Delhi as my real home.

I made quite a lot of friends there too. Where you decide to settle you are bound to make friendships with the other women who live there. But for people like us it was different from those who had been born and brought up in the city. Those who have been long resident there and possess their own house live a more settled life and can make more stable friendships. People like us who come in from the villages mostly lived alongside people of the same kind or with the refugees who had come into Delhi when Pakistan was created in 1947. Where houses and flats are taken on rent people are shifting all the time, and as soon as a neighbour moves house it is difficult to maintain the same relationship at a distance. If you live in a rented place your neighbours are changing all the time; people are constantly coming and going. So it was still with our relatives that we felt the closest ties.

At first I found city life very strange. The dialect of Delhi is quite different from that of my own village and I found it hard to understand at first. I felt very self-conscious of my country accent; I even felt shy of speaking to the untouchable woman who used to come every day to clean the toilets. When I heard her coming I would hide in the other room so that she would not know that I was there. I was afraid that if she spoke to me I would not understand what she had said and that she would laugh at me. And when it came to fetching the milk I was just as helpless. In the village we had had our own buffaloes, we had never had to go out and buy milk. I had not even any idea what the rate for milk would be and felt ashamed to confess my ignorance by asking. When the milkman came down the street all the other women ran out to buy from him but I lingered inside looking at the empty can and wondering what to do in my confusion. Fortunately my husband's elder brother's daughter was staying with us at the time and she said she would go and get the milk for me. When I saw how little milk she had got for the money I had given her I thought, 'Oh dear how ever shall I make do.' I had had no idea that it was so expensive. In the village we had always had not merely enough to drink our fill but sufficient to make curds and butter also.

It was when I came to Delhi that I first met with people from other parts of India, from outside the Punjab, and sometimes their customs seemed very strange to me. Where we first lived there was a Madrassi woman living in the same building. Now Madrassi people like to eat rice with their food, not *chapatties* like our Punjabi folk. Whatever vegetables they prepare – lentils, aubergines, tomatoes – they must have rice to go with them. Then they scrape it all up in balls with their fingers so that the juice runs down their fore-arms, not neatly with a piece of *chapatti* or a spoon. So one day I said to her, 'Look, why don't you eat like we do? After all, you are people of good family. Surely where you come from people don't eat like that?' She was very offended and abused me roundly, when I had only meant to tell her nicely that we didn't like to watch such messy eating.

Once I got accustomed to town life it was not long before I was so used to its conveniences and facilities that I no longer wished to return to the village. In the village I would have had to work so much harder, going to the well to wash the clothes, digging our own fields for vegetables. In Delhi, if we wanted vegetables all we had to do was to walk down to the market and buy them, all fresh and ready. In the cities people have more leisure to stroll about and enjoy themselves. All the women get together in the afternoon and swap ideas about the latest fashions. You are always up to date if you live in a town. And it was only after I came to Delhi that I started to wear a *sari*. In the villages of the Punjab the women mostly wear a *salvar-kamiz*; occasionally they wear a *sari* on special occasions after they are married, but only a few. But in Delhi I soon learnt how to tie a *sari*, although even now I still use a *salvar-kamiz* for everyday wear. When I used to go to my husband's village on visits my mother-in-law would be shocked at the way I dressed. 'Really, Satya,' she would say, 'Why don't you cover your head properly? A married woman should cover the whole of her head – not even her plait should show at the back. It is only modest.' Of course, in the towns the women at most just toss a scarf or the end of their *saris* over their heads and never mind how much hair shows behind. In the villages people are much more conservative in such matters but I could not be bothered to keep the village custom. I had got too used to city ways. Probably a woman who came from a really backward part of the countryside would have had more difficulty in adapting herself; those who come from the villages around Agra or Mathura must find Delhi even more strange than I did. But the Punjab is a richer area and people coming from there will not find Delhi so different from what they are used to as will people from the poorer districts.

Chapter 44

CITY AND VILLAGE

It was only when I came to Delhi that I saw really severe poverty for the first time. I think that there is more poverty in the cities than in our part of the countryside, in spite of all the conveniences of town life. Many poor villagers from the Rohtak area come into Delhi to look for work and I used to see their women folk – dressed in their big wide skirts and brightly-coloured shawls. They get work on the construction sites, carting loads of earth from one place to another on their heads. Sometimes the women even give birth to their babies while they are at work, on the very building sites themselves, if you please. No nurse or midwife for them – they can't afford it. Get nothing and you can give nothing. What can they do but pick up the baby and go home? And when they get there, what is the mother given to eat? Just millet bread. We are not rich people, but at least amongst our folk a new mother is made to rest and is given plenty of milk to restore her strength. Those poor women have to get up and go to work again almost the very next day, as though nothing had happened. See how poverty makes a slave out of a man. Many of the men can't get employment and in that case the wife just has to take the baby with her to work. When she gets there she gets on with her tasks, leaving her child on a blanket spread out under a tree. If the baby gets hungry she has nothing to give but her own milk. Over here they tell you, 'The baby must be given his bottle at such-and-such a time, at such-and-such a time he must have his orange juice.' Those people are human beings just like us, but who gives their babies orange juice to drink?

The trouble is that in India people in the cities depend entirely on wage labour. So long as they are in work they are all right, but the moment they are unemployed they are in trouble. In the village, if you have even a little land, your life is more secure. Your fields will yield a little grain and your neighbours will help you if you are in straits. There people take some responsibility for each other's welfare.

You may ask, 'Then why do people ever leave the village in the first place?' They go to the towns for the same reason that they leave India for London; they crave a more luxurious life and a fancier style of living.

So many boys from my own village have left and are sitting in the towns now, like my own two brothers for instance. Some boys from our village have even come to England. Quite a lot in fact have arrived here. The people of the village have become scattered and if I were to go back with my children now I would find few faces I would recognise. The girls I used to play with would all have gone to their husbands' villages and the boys would all have left for the towns.

We were always fortunate in that my husband was never out of work and earned fairly good pay. So long as you have work in the town you are all right, provided that you live as we did and do not fritter cash away on needless luxuries. As long as my sister and my brother-in-law were living with us they used to get rations on their names and we used to get our own on ours. We would share out what we had brought and seldom ran short of anything. I used to go and buy the grain every month and get it ground. Then the shop-keeper would deliver the sack to our house. At that time things were much less expensive than they are now. I am not sure exactly how things are these days as it is about five years since I left, you must remember. But a woman who had just arrived from India happened to visit us the other day and she was telling me that wheat has gone right up to Rs. 40 per *maund* in Delhi. These days there does not seem to be much difference in food prices between Delhi and London.

Chapter 45

'BABIES ARE WELCOMED INTO THE WORLD'

OF course once I had settled down with my husband I wanted to have children of my own more than anything else so I was very pleased when I became pregnant about three years after we got married. In India a girl usually goes to her parents' house to have her first baby and I set off to my father's village a month or so beforehand. I did not feel too nervous because I knew that there was a midwife in the village; there was even a little hospital not too far away. If a woman were in great pain or difficulty someone could pick her up and take her there from our village fairly easily.

Over there, they make a great fuss of a new mother, and everything is done to make things easy for her after her delivery. For a good while before Pritam was born my parents had begun to put by butter specially for me in a separate tin so that they would have it ready to feed me with after the baby came. People always do that; if a woman is having her baby at her husband's house then her mother-in-law will do the same. As soon as she knows her daughter-in-law is pregnant she will start to collect butter thinking, 'Our daughter-in-law will eat this when our grandchild is born.' So when Pritam arrived I was fed on butter and almonds. For the first two months I didn't eat ordinary *chapatties* with the rest of the family but had special food prepared for me separately – almonds, milk, sweets and all kinds of strength-giving things. People do that in India so that the mother can get her vigour back and so that she will be able to give a plentiful supply of milk for her baby.

And then for thirteen days I didn't have to stir from my bed. I did not even have to go outside to the toilet – someone would bring a pot so that I did not have to exert myself. And for a whole month I did not have to do any cooking. Amongst our Indian people it is said that the new mother of a baby is impure for thirteen days after the delivery. It is as though she were dirty. She is not allowed to go into the kitchen or to touch anything there. After thirteen days she gets up and takes a bath and then they hold the celebrations for the birth of the baby – at least they do if it is a boy. If it is a girl they don't do so much. So for thirteen days I just lay quietly on my bed and people brought me food and water there. On the thirteenth day I went into the kitchen and made a couple of fried cakes. That is the custom there; it shows that the mother is no longer impure and that now she can cook for the others.

When my first son was born there was much more celebration. In India people prefer boy babies to girl babies. I remember my mother-in-law had a quarrel with another woman in her village. That woman had two sons and those two sons each had sons only, no daughters. One had three boys, the other five. At that time I had borne only daughters. The first was Pritam and she, poor thing, was in bad health just as she is now. The second little girl died of fever at only eighteen months. So that woman used to taunt my mother-in-law that her son had no boys, only girls. I myself felt very sad after I lost that little girl and I felt that it was time that I had a baby boy. So when Sarinder was born we were all very pleased, not least my mother-in-law who could now answer that woman back. We were so happy that we sent a letter at once to my in-laws to tell them of the good news. They must have been watching the post very eagerly when they knew that my delivery time was near. Mind you, I don't think that one should boast of having boys. It is not to your own credit if you have more sons, because it was God who gave them to you; he decided whether they should be girls or boys, not you. If there are boys in the world then there must be girls in the world too, otherwise how will they get married? For myself, though I was very pleased to get my two sons, I never minded having daughters, and I can honestly say that I do not love my girls less because they are girls.

When Sarinder was born I did not go to my parents' house but stayed in Delhi. It was not the first baby, after all. In Delhi there are very good facilities and you can hire a nurse and midwife if you want to be delivered at home, or go to hospital if you prefer it that way. If you hire a nurse she will come round to your house beforehand to check that the room where you will be delivered is satisfactory, see that the light is all right, that there is water at hand, and that if the mother lives upstairs toilet facilities can be arranged for her so that she does not have to trail up and down stairs. If you hire a private nurse like that it will cost you about Rs. 25 to Rs. 30 according to how long you need her care. If the mother wants to keep the nurse longer she can give more, or if the baby is just delivered easily in a trice then she need give only Rs. 20. It just depends on the case.

So far as my case was concerned, my husband had a government job and the government provides special facilities for its employees in Delhi. We were registered in the health centre where we used to be able to get all the medicines we ever needed. If they were expensive then my husband would get the price refunded when his pay came if he showed the receipt. And we could hire a nurse from that centre without any charge at all, so we were well provided for. But though the nurse was sent free of charge we would still give her something as a token of gratitude and to show our happiness that the baby was delivered safely. When Asha was born we gave the nurse Rs. 2 and when Sarinder was born we gave Rs. 5. Even when Pappi was born over here we gave the nurse who attended me something. People over here do not need money so badly but we wanted to show how happy we were, so my husband spent about ten shillings on flowers for her. She was so pleased, she said she would put them beside her bed in the hostel where she lived so that she could enjoy looking at them.

In Delhi we had a midwife as well as a nurse. You can hire one there for Rs. 1 or Rs. 1½ a day. Just as the nurse is beneath the doctor in rank, so the midwife is beneath the nurse. As well as attending the birth she does work like changing the mother's bedding, making her clean and comfortable, combing her hair for her and washing her clothes. We always gave the midwife something extra as well of course to show our happiness. Sometimes people give her the baby's weight in rice; they put the baby on one side of the scales and the rice on the other and perhaps some flour and lentils also to take away with her.

I had so many friends and neighbours in Delhi and while I was confined to my bed after the delivery they would come to see me and look after me. They would make the food for the whole family until I was fit to use the kitchen again. I remember when Sarinder was born it was January and very cold indeed. My neighbours would come and light the stove for me and then sit round it warming their hands and chatting with me to keep me company. In fact we kept two stoves burning, it was so cold. We kept feeding them with big coals. We thought, 'Never mind the expense, it's not every day that a son is born in our house.' Where we were living at that time there were four apartments facing on to the one courtyard and I used to be very friendly with the women who shared the courtyard with us. They never left me alone for one minute while I was in bed after having Sarinder. Somebody or other would always be sitting there to look after me and get me anything I wanted. We would chat together or listen to the radio. In India there is always someone there to give you a hand when you need it and that is what I miss so sorely over here.

On the thirteenth day after Sarinder was born we had a big celebration. All the women in our quarter arrived to sing songs and to congratulate us, and everyone who came was given fine food to eat as well as sweets to take away. And five weeks after the birth we held another celebration for our relatives. That is the custom amongst our Punjabi people; a special celebration is held for the relatives, the celebrations on the thirteenth day are mainly for the members of the household and the people who live locally. After the birth of a son all the relatives are sent letters to tell them that a son has been born and they all arrive, bringing presents. The mother's parents will bring clothes for the new baby and gifts for her in-laws too – jewellery if they can afford it, but outfits of new clothes for everybody at the very least. The mother gets new bedding for her baby and a little cot to put him in. That is what happened when our first son was born. Of course, if the baby is a girl - or even if it is a boy when there are already many children in the family - then they give less; if you already have ten babies you do not expect such elaborate festivities when an eleventh arrives. But the mother's relatives will always bring something to mark the occasion, however little. Then the baby's parents will distribute sweets to everyone - again they don't give so much if it is a girl but at least they give something. When Pappi was born over here we sent Rs. 1,000 to my husband's brother in Delhi so that he could give everyone *laddus* on our behalf. We are far from our family so we could not do all that we wanted to do but when we go back then we shall hold a celebration over there and do everything properly to make up for it. All the same, when Pappi was born we held a *path* in thanksgiving and on his first birthday we held a *kirtan*. Each time we invited all our friends and gave them a really good dinner. We didn't invite anyone this year on his birthday; it is too much trouble to invite a large number of people over here and feed them all. In India so many people are around to help you cook the food and serve it, but here you have to do everything on your own. But it is only right and proper that you should do something to show your gratitude and happiness when you have cause for rejoicing in your household, isn't it?

I had both Sarinder and Asha at home whilst I was living in Delhi. In India things are made easy for a woman if she has a baby at home; I never had a baby in hospital until I came here. But if you want to go to hospital in Delhi you can do so very easily. The hospitals in Delhi are very good in my opinion, perhaps even better than over here. After all over here they only give you one post-natal check-up after six weeks but there you have to come to the hospital two or three times at fortnightly intervals after the baby is born. And it is not too dear for people like us to get a private room if we want one. There you can have a phone in your room to telephone your family whenever you want to, your own heater and a stove to make tea. Your relatives can come any time they like so long as they get a pass made. I have seen the private rooms they have in Delhi hospitals because when my sister-in-law's daughter was ill she had one. She had to be isolated from the other patients because of the danger of infection. It is very comfortable to have your own room.

In India each baby is welcomed into the world however many there are in the family already and I think that people love their children more over there. Here of course, they don't beat their children; they discipline them less but they love them less. They turn them out of the house early so that they can get to work on time and the poor children have to play outside in the cold if they get back from school before their parents are home from work. As soon as they are old enough they throw them out and say, 'Now go and earn some money.' In India people do everything for their children. If they can't afford jewellery for themselves, at least they will see that their daughters get it. If one of my children expresses a desire for any particular thing, I will always do my best to get it, cost what it may. I should never like any of my children to hope for something and to have that hope unfulfilled. If there is anything my children don't like to eat then I don't prepare it in my house. If we ever had too little food, then the children would eat first. In this way the children get attached to their parents. If my children know that I will do everything that is in my power for them, then because of this trust they will cling to me. As they get bigger they will come to know that we will get them married and provide everything at their marriages. In England parents give less to their children, I suppose because they know that sooner or later they will leave home and live on their own or make their own marriages. After all, the government will look after the parents in their old age. But in India there is much more affection between parents and children.

Chapter 46

VISITING THE VILLAGE

WHEN I was newly married I used to go to visit my parents quite a lot. If my village had been nearer I would have gone even more often. If your mother lives just round the corner you can go to see her any time you like; a rickshaw costs only about eight *annas*. But our village is a long way from Delhi and it is a tedious journey. We would get the train to Phillaur where we would arrive late at night. We would then have to stay overnight there and take the bus the next morning to the village. So we would not arrive until noon of the day after we had set out. Sometimes I would stay two days, three days, according to how long my husband could spare me. My mother used to be so happy to see me – what mother would not be glad to see her daughter?

But after my brother had come to settle in Delhi I used to visit my old home less often. It was simpler for my father to come to Delhi himself and meet us all while he was there – me, my brother and my younger sister. What should I have done in the village when most of the young children who were only so high when I got married had grown beyond recognition? I did not feel like making the long journey on my own and if I felt like going I would say to my sister, 'Come along with me, I can't go alone.'

After my children were born I sometimes used to take them to my parents' house for visits. One day, I remember, we got a letter to say that my father was sick. My brother went off immediately and I thought that I had better go also. But my son Sarinder was at school and his holidays were still a fortnight away, so I knew I could not take him with me. I left him with my sister and took Asha with me. When my father had recovered and I was ready to return she did not want to come back to Delhi with me, she liked the village so much. I had to make a second trip later in order to collect her. And when we were just about to come to England I left her with my parents for another stay; I was very busy with all the preparations for coming here, getting the passports and papers ready, so I sent her to the village for a few days. She used to love the place, and would roam around so contentedly.

My younger sister was still at home at that time (she was newly married and had not yet gone to her husband's house) and when she went to milk the buffaloes Asha used to tag along with her. My sister would give her a beaker of warm milk fresh from the udder. As she drank it she would get it all over her face and then say, 'Look at my white moustache!' When they asked her if she didn't want to go home she used to say, 'No, I don't want to go back to Delhi. Tell my Mummy to come here and see me, and remind her to bring some mangoes when she comes.' She was so happy in the village. But then what child is not happy when it is surrounded with love and affection? Children only become homesick and unhappy when you ill-treat them.

As for my husband's village, I visited it very seldom. What would we do over there anyway? I had not been brought up there, I did not know who was who like I did in my parents' village. Most Indian sons bring their wives to live with their parents but in our case we were living apart from the very beginning and I never got to know my husband's village at all. If someone in the family happened to be going there they would ask me if I wanted to go along with them, but I seldom did. We had come to regard Delhi as our home, not my in-laws' village. There was nothing to draw us there – we owned no property, no land or house of our own there, and the more I got accustomed to Delhi the less I felt inclined to stir from my own little household.

But my parents-in-law used to come and see us quite frequently. When my mother-in-law felt bored or heavy-hearted she would come and visit us for a change. Then she would spend a month, two months with us before going home to the village again. I got on with her very well on the whole. She was not a quarrelsome woman and that's the main thing in a mother-in-law, isn't it? She could not play the old game of playing off one daughter in law against the other anyway, because the other daughter-in-law was my own sister.

In fact I visited my husband's village so seldom that I never really got to know the place at all. Old men and babies, they were all equally strangers to me. I would hardly know my way to my in-laws' house even to-day. You know, it is the custom in India for a married woman to veil her face from the older men in her husband's village, or at least from those who are his relatives. Well, I did not even know who was a relative and who wasn't, who was older and who was younger. Once I went with my elder brother-in-law's daughter – I intended to make an offering of Rs. 50 at a temple in the neighbourhood. If someone came along the path she would nudge me and say, 'Aunty, so-and-so is coming.' And I would say, 'Well, how am I supposed to know so-and-so when I never saw him in my life before?' I had no idea as to whom I could show my face to and from whom I should hide it so I usually did not bother. I could not be expected to know who was who, and so no one could criticise me. For that matter they had just as little idea as to who I might be, so they didn't feel any grievance anyway. It is only if you settle in a place for a time that people get to know that you are so-and-so's daughter-in-law.

Once, I remember, I had to go to my in-laws' village to attend a funeral. That same niece's husband had died, and it is the custom in India when anyone dies for all the women to come and commiserate with the widow, to weep and mourn with her. If I had not gone too it would have been considered very remiss of me, so I had to go even though I knew the people there so slightly. Fortunately my husband has a cousin who lives in Delhi and his wife looked after me while we were there in the village. She was very kind and thoughtful and would show me around the place, where to go to the toilet and so forth. I would just follow her about.

When I came to attend my mother-in-law's funeral I nearly

got lost on the way. When I got off the train I asked somebody the way, and he kindly offered to accompany me for as
far as his route coincided with mine. We walked together for a
few miles but at the next village he had to leave me as he had
some business there and I had to go on alone. There was a big
gurudvara there and he had been on his way to visit it. I soon
got properly lost and very tired too, as I was carrying Sarinder
in my arms. He was just a little baby of three months at that
time. Just then I met a little boy so I called out to him,
'Brother, if you know the way please take me to such-and-such
a village and I will give you some money.' He agreed so I
picked up Sarinder and trudged after him. I was relieved when
the village came into sight and I gave him eight *annas* and
dismissed him. But that was not the end of my problems that
day. In India it is the custom when arriving at a house of
mourning for the women to start keening and wailing some
way down the road, before they reach the house itself, and to
keep on as they walk up to it. Then the people inside know
that someone has come to pay their condolences. But exactly
where you should begin to weep and wail depends on the local
custom. Now I come from the Punjab and the general custom
is the same all over the Punjab, but the details vary from village
to village. For instance if I had been going to a funeral in my
own village I should have thought, 'Right, now I have passed
so-and-so's house, or such-and-such a tree, I should begin
weeping now.' And exactly at that spot I should have started
up. But in my in-laws' village I had no idea where it would be
considered appropriate to begin. In a large village not everyone knows automatically why you have come and it would
have looked silly if I had started weeping too far outside the
village. People would have said, 'What is she doing, a grown
woman carrying on like that? What can be the matter with her?'
Suppose you were going to a funeral at Southall, the people in
Aldgate would think you were crazy if you started wailing all
the way down the high street there. But if you leave it too late,
people might think you were disrespectful to the dead or un-
sympathetic to the mourners. I was just trying to make a

guess as to where was the best place to start when I heard my sister's voice calling from some way off. 'Oh, look! There is Satya just coming down the path.' So I started to weep and wail immediately because I knew that I must be pretty near the house. I was relieved when I arrived and found that I had not offended anyone.

Chapter 47

FATHER-IN-LAW AND DAUGHTER-IN-LAW

AFTER my mother-in-law's death my father-in-law was left all alone so we asked him to come to Delhi to live with us, and in fact he stayed with us until we left India. When we came here we suggested that he go to my younger brother-in-law's house, which he agreed to, and he stayed there until he died. In India sons look after their parents when they get old, they don't abandon them like they do here. They give them much respect, and so do the daughters-in-law. There it is considered right if your husband's aged parents are living with you to attend to their every need with great care. There is sense in this, because old people are helpless like babies, they cannot do everything for themselves. But a baby can do no more than cry if it does not get its milk at the right time because it does not know how to talk. An old man can not only use his tongue, he will quarrel and abuse the other people in the house if he does not get what he wants.

I was never in a position to serve my mother-in-law because all the time we were in Delhi she was living in the village. That is where she died, poor woman. But when my father-in-law came to live with us, I did my best to see that he was properly looked after. A married woman in India does not have too much to say to her father-in-law as a rule; she must veil her face from him and behave in a very subdued manner in his presence. But I always got on very well with my father-in-law as my respect for him was genuine and he was a good man. When he got older his legs became very stiff and he could not walk easily so when he went to have his daily bath I would fill his bucket at the tap myself and take it up to the bathroom for him. I would even massage his legs and bring him oil to rub on his body. Twenty times a day he would say, 'May you both prosper, my children. May God give you all you desire.' And we would try to satisfy his slightest want. Who has time to run around after the whims of old people in this country? If he said he fancied this, that, or the other we would say, 'Right, we will get it.' In the afternoon, at about three o'clock, I would go to the market and fetch bananas for him. Or sometimes he would fancy dates or guavas. We were able to do this because at that time God did indeed give us much to be thankful for. My husband had secure employment and we could afford to keep open house.

My father-in-law liked Delhi. He had come fresh from the village like I had, and everything was novel to him. He would go out and stroll about when he pleased. He could not talk to people much or make friends outside the home because he could only talk our local dialect and in Delhi the main language is Hindi, but he was quite contented. I don't regret our decision not to bring him over here with us. He would never have been happy here. For one thing, he would have felt the cold acutely. He would have nothing to do all day and no one to keep him company while we were at work. We would have had to say to him each morning, 'There, old man, you just stay sitting there until we come back to-night.' What would he have thought of such a life after the way he lived with us in Delhi? Old people need such special care and I think it is cruel to drag them here if you are not going to be able to give it to them.

Chapter 48

RENTING A HOUSE

IN India when people say that they have taken a 'house' they do not necessarily mean that they have the whole building to themselves. A 'house' could mean an apartment of two, three, four rooms, or perhaps only one room. They may have a bathroom to themselves or they may have to share it with other families living in the same building. The same goes for the latrine, although in the newer colonies in Delhi all the houses that are being built nowadays each have their own separate flush toilet. We lived in several different places in Delhi during the time we spent there, but they mostly consisted of one room with a kitchen. But we always had our own courtyard where we could sleep outdoors in the hot weather or enjoy the mid-day sunshine in the winter.

The government provides quarters for its employees in Delhi and when my husband went into government service we were lucky enough to get such a place. It was so convenient; if anything went wrong you just had to report it and they would arrange for it to be put right straight away. You just had to tell them to come at a particular time. Or if the place needed redecorating they would inform us as to which day they were sending the workmen round. Then we would clear all our belongings out and stack them in the courtyard. They would come along and in no time at all the painting would be finished. In one day they used to do all the decorating and repairs and then when they had gone we could wash down the floors, put back all our things and sit down in comfort.

If you ask me, I think that Indian houses are better than English houses on the whole. Here the climate is such that a hundred things can go wrong and the place is always needing repairs. If you leave your house for a while without inspecting it, you will find it full of woodworm at the end of only six months. The walls get damp, and as people here cover their walls with paper instead of whitewash, the paper gets dirty and needs renewing practically every year. And the landlords take ages to get these things done. That has been our experience at least. Landlords here could not care less about the conditions their tenants live in. In India the houses are well built and will stand for a lifetime without needing much done to them. People there are closer to their neighbours and if you have to leave your house empty for some time for any reason your next door neighbour will keep an eye on it for you to see that the monsoon rain does not leak in.

In Delhi you could rent a house at that time for Rs. 100 per month. We only paid Rs. 4 per month because the house had been owned by some Muslims who had fled to Pakistan in 1947. Houses like that are in the hands of the public custodian and are rented out at low rates to government employees. We only had to pay a nominal rent and that made it much easier for us because rent is the major expense in the cities in India; in the villages you only have to pay a few rupees a month to get a fine spacious house all to yourself.

We kept open house and it was seldom that we did not have someone staying with us. That is another difference between this country and India. Over there, if you rent rooms, no one asks how many people you have staying there or whether they are paying you rent. No one asks you anything. Mind you, I don't like overcrowding as a rule, but it is good to feel free to help a relative or friend when they need accommodation.

Chapter 49

'THE PROPER LIFE FOR A WOMAN'

I NEVER used to go out to work in India; very few uneducated women do. Here a woman can get a job any time she likes in one of the factories or laundries but in Delhi hardly any factories employ women. Very conservative people don't like women to go out to work. People who come from the villages would say, 'But if our wives go out to work, and while they are at work their father-in-law or someone comes along, how can they drop whatever they are doing in order to veil their faces?' That is why they don't like women to go out too much. All the same, in the cities this custom of veiling one's face is changing nowadays, and in Delhi women move around with every freedom; in the towns people do not know the folk they live amongst as well as they do in the villages, so no one cares whether the women veil their faces or not, and the women think, 'Nobody knows me so why should I bother?' In some families married women even treat their fathers-in-law with the same familiarity as they would their own fathers; they sit and chat with them, eat together and even go to the cinema together. We don't do that in my family, but customs are changing so fast in Delhi that there will soon be hardly any difference between Delhi and London. The only difference will be that the ladies speak Hindi in the one city and English in the other.

All the same, there are still only a few opportunities for paid work for women over there, so that most women just stay at home quietly and look after their children, taking them to school in the morning, fetching them home at night, and generally leading a peaceful life. That is the proper life for a woman; none of this rush and bustle in the morning to get the baby to the baby-minder on time, get the children ready for school on time and get to the factory oneself on time. If you saw the life women like me lead over there you would say: 'That is the way to live, that is really easy living.'

I will tell you what I did every day. I would get up early in the morning – about six o'clock – and bath myself. Then I would generally go to the temple and spend a little time there. When I got back I would sit down quietly and start cooking. I would make a vegetable curry and some *chapatties* for my husband's lunch and put them into his lunch box. He used to go to work on a cycle and I would strap the lunch box on to the back of the cycle all ready for him to set off. He would leave at about eight and after I had given the children their breakfast and taken them to school I would give the house a thorough cleaning, or sometimes I would wash a few clothes in the courtyard. Often I would join the other women who were my neighbours and we would wash our clothes together, laughing and chatting all the while. There was a factory near our house where a whistle was sounded at eleven o'clock each day to tell the workers it was time for their break. So we would work until we heard the whistle blow and then finish what we were doing and go indoors. I would take another bath then if it was the hot season, and shut the door quietly so as to take a little rest. I would lie down and put the radio on and often even while it was playing I would feel drowsy and fall asleep. I would not get up until three when I would wash my hands and face, comb and plait my hair and put on a clean *sari* or *salvar* before going to fetch the children. Sarinder had been at school for four years when we left India. Whatever was the name of the school? I have forgotten completely. And I am afraid he has forgotten all the Hindi he ever learnt there too, poor boy. It might be difficult for him if we ever went back because now Hindi is the national language and he would be at a disadvantage if he did not know it.

Asha was too young to go to school while we were in India, but she used to go to nursery when she was three or four years old. My neighbour's children used to go to the same nursery, and as we were quite friendly we used to go to collect our children together. Then one day I had an idea and I said to her, 'Look, why do we both need to go? I will take the children in the morning and you collect them in the afternoon.' So she said, 'All right, I will go in the afternoon.' That is how we used to help each other out. Well, one day she went to fetch the children and there was a new teacher who had only just started working there. My friend was standing outside waiting for our children to come out but after a long time Asha had still not appeared, so she asked the teacher, 'Are there any more children inside? My neighbour's little girl, Asha, has not come out yet.' The teacher said, 'I am new here so I don't know all the children's names yet. I don't know which one is Asha but you can go inside yourself and have a look. See if you can recognise her.' Well, my friend went in and had a good look round; in the end she spotted Asha curled up fast asleep on a mat. She had been fast asleep all the afternoon. What do little children of that age know of time? They are not ready to learn anything when they are so little. Wait until they develop some sense and then you can teach them.

After the children had come from school I would go to the market to buy fruit and vegetables and then sit down to make the evening meal. After we had eaten, sometimes we would say to each other, 'Come on, let's go for a stroll.' And we would take a turn outside in the cool of the evening before going to sleep. Life was so calm over there, everything was done at a leisurely pace – even our work.

Chapter 50

DIVERSIONS

YES, it was a leisurely life I led in Delhi. But it was not dull, either, as we had plenty of amusements. Sometimes there would be a wedding in the neighbourhood and I would put on my best clothes and jewellery and go along with the other women. In our country the custom is like this; in your own courtyard you can sit around in any old clothes you like, but when you go out you must dress up. If there was a wedding I would put on a nice new *sari*, my best bangles, gold ear-rings and necklace. All the women would put on all their jewellery before stepping outside their house on such occasions. And why is that? Because if you go to a wedding without putting on all your gold and finery you will be put to shame. Everybody will be decked out and they will say, 'Dear, dear, what sort of pauper is she married to that she can't afford to make herself look nice?'

If my husband was busy at work I would go out with the children on my own, or with the other women, but if he was free he would often take us out for a treat at the weekends. Sometimes we would go to see a film in the evening, but more often we would go to some temple taking the children along with us. There was a temple to the goddess Devi in Delhi which we used to visit frequently. Outside the temple there used to be a man who sold sweets for people to take inside to offer to the goddess. Or from the same stall you could buy a little iron tray all ready furnished with the things needed for worship – a lamp, flowers, sweets and incense. We used to pay four *annas* for one of these trays and then take it inside. In the temple we would bow down before the image of the goddess and offer the sweets and flowers we had bought, then light the lamp and burn the incense before her. Then the priest would give us some sweets to take away as *prasad*. Or sometimes we would provide food for little girls, feeding them in the name of the goddess. I would prepare lots and lots of fried cakes and pudding and take them to the temple to give to the girls there. We would make all the girls who had been invited sit down in a line and give them the food with our own hands. Sometimes we would feed as many as a hundred at once. People in India look on this as an act of charity. Occasionally on a Sunday we would pay a visit to the Birla *mandir* or to the Shish Ganj *gurudvara*. They are very famous and lots of people go to worship there. Generally I would take the children along too, or else I would leave them with my sister to look after. Some weekends we would go to one place, on others to another place, but I always used to enjoy these outings. But even during the week hardly a day would go by but I would pay a visit to one of the temples or *gurudvaras* near to our house, usually with the other women who were my neighbours.

Chapter 51

'INDIA IS SUCH A BIG PLACE'

ONCE we were settled in Delhi we did not leave it often except to visit our parents. We used to go on excursions within the city itself if we wanted to amuse ourselves. I had been to Amritsar once or twice and other places in the Punjab where there are big temples to visit, but otherwise I had seen nothing of India apart from Delhi and our Punjab. So, just before he was due to come to England, my husband said one day, 'Come on, I will take you for a holiday before I go. Let's go to see Agra. Then from Agra we can go to Brindaban. There are lots of holy places there and you will enjoy yourself.' The journey was not very pleasant – have you ever seen third class railway compartments in India? People have to climb over each other to get in and out at the stations, they are so crowded. Old men, little children, all get squeezed and trampled in the crush. But once we arrived, we enjoyed ourselves. First we went to Agra and took a look at the Taj Mahal. Then after Agra we visited Mathura and Brindaban – that is where the god Krishna was born on earth. Thousands of pilgrims had come there because it was the time of the festival of Janam Ashtami, Krishna's birthday. Crowds of people had come to see the temples. And there are so many temples over there. In some of the temples you might see hundreds of women gathered. Mostly they would be widows who had devoted themselves to a life of piety in their widowhood, and they would all be dressed in white with their heads shaved. That is the custom for widows in that part of India, it seems. I was amazed to see so many of them. They would all be sitting down with holy scripture books in their hands which they would be reading piously.

Something happened while we were staying in Agra which would make you laugh. I had taken several of my best print *saris* with me to wear; we used to go out every day either sight-seeing or visiting the temples and I wanted to look smart. We were staying in a *saran* – that is a kind of inn, usually attached to a temple, with a custodian who takes contributions from the visitors and pilgrims, who are provided with a bed and shelter for the night. One day all my *saris* had got dirty and I decided to wash them in the *saran*. I had a bath and then changed into a *salvar-kamiz*, having spread the clean *saris* in the sun to dry. When my husband came along, the custodian of the *saran* stopped him and said, 'Look here, brother, this is not the way to behave in a *saran*, in the vicinity of a temple.' My husband was surprised and said to him, 'Whatever do you mean? What have I done?' 'Look,' said the custodian, 'Yesterday you had that lady who was wearing the *sari* with you and now you have picked up some Punjabi woman and brought her here. This sort of thing won't do, you know.' Then my husband under-stood what the man meant and he laughed. 'But that is the same lady as you saw yesterday. She is my wife. Sometimes she wears a *sari* and sometimes a *salvar-kamiz*. Did you think it was a different woman? The only thing different was her clothes.' How we laughed! The people over there are not used to seeing women wear the *salvar-kamiz* and they thought I looked strange. They regard us Punjabis as rich people because the people who live in the villages in that part of India are much more backward and poor than our villagers in the Punjab.

Their customs are different from ours in some ways. For instance they are very particular about the way they eat. Of course we always wash our hands when we eat, but if they go outside their own home anywhere they don't consider themselves pure enough to sit down to their supper until they have had a good bath on their return and changed their clothes. Now, when we used to go out for the day, I would take a little shoulder bag with me – I remember that bag, it was a nice shade of almond colour – I used to pack a bottle of water or milk and a little food in it, so that if the children got hungry or thirsty while we were out, I could just open the bag and give them something. But when he saw this, the custodian of the *saran* was very shocked. 'Dear, dear,' he said, 'Do you really like to eat like that, food you have dragged around with you all day? We only like to eat in our own kitchen and then only when we have taken a proper bath.' I explained to him that the bag was just a matter of convenience – after all why should the poor children go hungry or thirsty? – and we were also quite particular when we were at home. But people in that part of India are very conservative. This made me realise that India is such a big place. People differ a lot in the kind of customs they observe from place to place. Now English people don't differ amongst themselves in their ways, but in India every province is different. If I went to Madras or Bengal I wouldn't understand one word of what the people there were saying.

Chapter 52

'A DIFFICULT TIME'

THAT was the last bit of pleasure I was to have for some while because after my husband left for England I went through a difficult time. So many problems began to trouble me and I had to deal with them all alone. I had not opposed my husband's going to England. He had been talking of going for some years. We always discuss everything together and when he asked me my opinion I said that I was quite happy about the idea. 'Don't worry,' I said, 'I am quite ready to go.' Not that I had ever felt that we lacked money; I was quite content living the way we did in Delhi. But I thought that if he would be happier working in England then it might be better for us to emigrate there. In any case the children would have the chance to learn English and get a really good education and better themselves. So I did not raise any objection.

Soon his passport and voucher were ready, and then I must admit that I started to feel a little nervous. It is not a small matter in India to leave government employment when you have a record of sixteen years' service. Government employment carries so many advantages there, especially the pension which my husband had now forfeited by leaving at that time. 'Now we have thrown away sixteen years' service, all for the sake of going to England. Who knows but this will turn out to be a serious mistake, curse it all?' I thought. But I kept my doubts to myself as it was too late to undo what we had already done.

But these doubts were only momentary for I thought that England was bound to be a good place to live. You see, I had barely any idea of what England was like or what difficulties we would face when we got there. In India everyone thinks of

England as a very rich country. All we knew was that those people who went to work there always came back loaded with money. So why should we not be able to go and do the same for ourselves? And all the English people we had ever seen in India had been rich. I never knew any white people myself in Delhi but there were plenty of English and American people living there. One Sunday I remember we had gone to the Shish Ganj *gurudvara* and were strolling about the streets afterwards. A lot of English people used to go there and shop in the *bazar*, and we used to watch them. But they really had no idea of the right way to buy things at all. If they bought a thing they would allow themselves to be cheated or would fail to take their change even when the shopkeeper offered it to them. That day I was watching a *Mem* buy some bananas. She could not speak our language so she did not know that she should ask for '*kele*' but she managed to make the shopkeeper understand what it was that she wanted. She asked for a dozen, picked them up and gave the man a one rupee note. Now the bananas were six *annas* a dozen, so out of one rupee she should have got back ten *annas*, isn't that so?

But she walked off without taking any change. The shopkeeper called out after her but of course she could not understand what he was saying. I suppose she must have thought that she had made an excellent bargain to have got as many as twelve bananas for one rupee since they are so expensive here in England. Or perhaps she just did not understand the Indian currency. But I remember thinking to myself at the time, 'These English people are either very generous or very foolish, but at all events they must come from a rich country indeed to be able to scatter their money around like that.'

Of course I had heard from other people that there is only one language in England and that is English, so I knew that we should have to learn some English if we were to go and live there. But I did not think it would be necessary to learn more than a little in order to get by, and I did not doubt that I would be capable of doing this. And I had also been told that the Indians who are already settled in England assist those who are newly arrived from India and help them out of their difficulties. So I did not anticipate that we should have any serious problems or worries in England. I was quite ignorant about the place, but then I had never been there myself, only heard other people talk about it, and you can't know all about something you have never seen with your own eyes, can you?

We stayed on in the same house which we had already been occupying after my husband left. There was no need to move as the rent was only four rupees a month. Gita and Baldev moved into that house when we left and are still there to this day. My husband used to send me money from England, although we had not by any means been left penniless when he went away because he had always been in the habit of putting some of his pay straight into the savings bank each month before bringing the rest home. So we had quite a bit of money saved up apart from what he had spent on his fare. We were never people of extravagant tastes and I also used to put away a little cash from time to time. It is a good thing to be thrifty because you never know what the future will bring, or at what time you may find yourself in need of money.

Once my husband had left us, nothing seemed to go right. The children missed him so much and used to cry for him all the time. Then my father-in-law fell ill – he was still living with us at that time – and his leg started to give him trouble again. On top of all these troubles I received a letter from my sister-in-law's daughter, Taro, to say that she was ill in hospital in Pagvara and would I go to see her? Now this girl was the daughter of my husband's dead sister. Her father had married again and her stepmother had never cared for the poor girl very much, and so she had had an unhappy childhood. She had always put her hope in the future, thinking that when she was married she would have her own husband and household and live a happy life. But those whose fate does not hold happiness will never be happy. I had brought her to Delhi and got her admitted to one of the biggest hospitals there for an operation. For three or four years she must have been staying with us in Delhi on and off, and during that time I came to love her dearly.

Her parents only asked us to send her back because they needed her help in the house when her stepmother was confined. After she got married her life was no better. She fell ill again and her in-laws did not take any care for her health and neither would her father do anything. He said, 'Now she is married she is not my responsibility any longer.' I had heard that she was ill and unhappy but I was perplexed as to what I should do. If I approached either her father or her in-laws they might think that she had been complaining to me and make her life even more miserable for her. So we just wrote, 'Taro, what has happened to you? We have not heard from you for a long time. Try to write to us from time to time and let us know how you are.' That hint gave her the opportunity to tell us the whole story if she wished, and that was when I received her letter. She wrote, 'I am very sick and in no state to do anything. I don't know what will become of me.' I told her to come at once, either alone or with someone to accompany her, according to her condition, but at any rate to come to us at all costs. I knew there was no help to be expected from her in-laws. So often it happens like that in India – everyone in the family likes the new daughter-in-law until she falls ill and has to spend a few days in bed or needs expensive treatment. Then they have no more use for her and say to her father, 'Now you look after your daughter yourself.' Taro's husband brought her to our house and I saw that she was very ill, the poor girl could hardly draw breath. So I took her along as soon as possible to get her admitted to the hospital. When they had settled her in her bed there her husband made ready to leave for his home. He was afraid that she would die and that if she died while he was there with us he would have to pay for all the expenses of the funeral. I told him straight out, 'Look here, Taro is your wife, she is your responsibility. You should stay on for a few days here at least until you see that she is on the mend.' I don't know how many injections they gave her but I do know that they took several pounds of poisonous fluid from her stomach where the stitches from her previous operation had broken and become infected. When she had recovered a bit Taro went home but it was not long before she fell ill again. I got word from a relative that she had been abandoned in Pagvara hospital; it seemed her father-in-law had washed his hands of her. I got her moved to Delhi once again. It was a Saturday when she arrived and the following Thursday she died. I sent a telegram to her in-laws but they showed no concern except to send Rs. 15 to cover the cost of the funeral. I had to do everything myself, my husband being away. It was I who had her body taken down to the cremation ground and when we got there the funeral priest told us that as there was no very close relative present that person who had loved her the most ought to be the one to ignite the funeral pyre. So it was I who had to do this, although my heart rebelled so that I could hardly bring myself to set light to the wood. All the while she had been in hospital I had wept every time I saw her and I even used to cry on the way home from the hospital. I had never experienced such troubles and sorrows as during that year when my husband was in England.

And when I received his letters they were full of his own problems. At first he used to write to me that he was so homesick and so worried about whether he would be able to get work or not that he could not sleep at night. All night he would lie awake thinking, 'When shall I see my little children again? What must they be doing at this moment? And what can they be thinking of a father who has left them like this?' He could neither sleep nor eat, he wrote, so how could I give him another cause for grief and regret by burdening him with our troubles too?

And then when he did get work he found it so strenuous, since by that time his health had weakened also. 'Here the people who are uneducated have to work like donkeys, yet what other work am I qualified to do except manual work?' he used to write to me. The people in whose house he was living considered him fair game as he did not have his family with him in England to support. 'Rampal can afford to eat curds with his curry.' That is what they would say, and then charge him four pounds a week in rent. So naturally he was worried as we had thought that he would be able to save up enough money to enable us to join him in only a few months. When he used to write that he was miserable in England I used to think, 'Yes, it is certainly a matter for misery – you have left a good job where you used to get nearly Rs. 200, the home you had established and the comfortable life we used to lead here only to be miserable in England.' But I kept quiet about my own regrets and troubles and just looked forward to the time when we would be able to be together again. When you have someone to help you and stand by you in life then you can comfort each other. There is no use in having thousands of rupees if you have no helpmate. If you lie sick with a fever and you cry out for water, will your rupees get up and fill your glass for you? So I thought to myself, 'What is the use of thinking about whether we shall be richer or poorer in England. Let us just be together as a family again.' So now you will see why I was quite relieved to be leaving Delhi, where I had always been so happy before, and to go to join my husband in a foreign country.

Chapter 53

A LONG JOURNEY

My father came to see us off at the airport, travelling from the village especially for the purpose. My brother and younger sister were already in Delhi of course and they came too, so we had a good send-off. I had not packed many things to take with us, just some bedding and a few clothes for the children. My husband had told me that there was no need to bother to bring everything as anything we needed could be bought in London when we arrived. Also I was not sure how much we would be allowed to bring through the customs. 'Anyway,' I thought to myself, 'I am quite good at sewing. I can always borrow someone's machine and run up a few clothes for us if we need any more.'

The passengers on the plane were mainly Europeans, there were only one or two Indians besides ourselves. When they brought food round to the passengers I wanted to get some for the children but I was not sure whether the price of the meal was included in what we had paid for the ticket or if there was a separate charge, and knowing no English I couldn't ask. Fortunately there was an Indian in the seat in front of mine so I said to him, 'Brother, do we have to pay for the food separately?' He explained to me that the meal was in fact covered by the price of the ticket.

Our plane stopped in Moscow on the way here. We did not have to change, it was just to give us all a rest. I had been sitting right at the back of the plane and it took me some time to make my way down to the front with the children, and by the time I managed to get off everyone else had disappeared. There was an official standing there asking to see our passports. 'Passports,' I understood so I showed him ours and then started looking round to see where all the other passengers had gone. We seemed to have been left behind. Then I saw that they were all sitting in a coach, so I got into the coach too and it took us to the airport building where there was a restaurant. As soon as the coach stopped all the others trooped off to have tea. I did not know how to ask for anything so I did not like to follow them. I sat down to one side feeling rather confused. When they all came back again after having their tea I followed the crowd back to the coach again. They started checking from a list that everyone had arrived and when they were sure that no one had been left behind the aeroplane took off again. When we got off at London I just followed everyone else again, copying what they were doing. A man started to ask for my passport again – he must have been some sort of official – and then he said something which I did not understand. The Indian I had met in the plane explained to me that he was asking me how many children I had, so I told him the names of my three children and then he left me alone. We didn't have any trouble because after all they were all my own children, weren't they? I wasn't trying to smuggle someone else's children into the country. I just kept quiet and followed everyone else. Then a lady asked us for copies of our vaccination certificates. Well, I understood this time because I caught the words 'injections' and 'copy'. People use these English words in India, don't they? So I had heard them before and guessed what she meant. I showed her the certificates and she let us through. Outside that building a man was standing and he was saying something to me, but I could not understand a word. How could I tell what he was saying? I felt very shy and confused. Then I saw all the bags lined up and guessed that he was asking me to pick out the ones which were ours. So I pointed to our bags and he took them to where the cars and taxis were standing. And that was when I saw my husband standing waiting for us with his friend. I was shocked to see how ill and thin he looked. His complexion looked dull and his face pinched. Yet we were so glad to see each other, and I knew that he would recover now that we were all together again.

Chapter 54

A NEW LIFE

WE sat ourselves down in my husband's friend's car and drove home. (Home meant the room in someone's house where my husband was living at that time.) I was looking out of the window in amazement all the way. Everything seemed so different; the people, their clothes, the houses, even the trees looked different from those we had been used to see in India.

We only stayed a short time in that room because my husband wanted something more spacious for us, and after eight days we shifted to rooms where we must have stayed for nearly a year. These rooms were over an Indian grocery stores and we were the only tenants so there was no one to tell us what to do or what not to do.

During those first weeks in England I felt curiosity to look at everything outside because it was so different from India. Yet I also felt shy and frightened. For the first month I did not even dare answer the door if someone knocked while my husband was out at work. I did not know a word of English, how would I have known what to say or what to do? 'Hush,' I would tell the children, 'Someone is knocking. Keep your voices down and tread lightly, and they will think that no one is at home and go away.' From what I have seen since it is always like that for Indian women who come here, at least during their first few weeks.

As long as my husband was out at work I did not stir from the house. If I needed any food during the day I would just run downstairs to the shop and get what I wanted. But of course one needs other things for the family besides groceries. So one day my husband said, 'Come along and I will show you how to do the shopping.' First we went to buy the children some warm coats, because the clothes we had brought from India were not thick enough. Next we went to Woolworth's, I remember. And then we went to a supermarket. I was amazed to see such a huge shop, not at all like the *bazars* where I had done my shopping in India. It seemed funny to take a little basket instead of asking the shop-keeper for what we wanted. Yet what a lot we managed to cram into that little basket that day! We filled it right up. I went one or two times more with my husband and then I felt confident enough to go alone. After all, if I was not sure about the name of anything I had to ask for I could always ask the woman in the shop what the word for such-and-such an item was in English and she would tell me. It had been very inconvenient, having to wait until my husband was free before going shopping since at that time he was working overtime on both Saturday and Sunday and had hardly any time to spare.

The trouble which most Indian women like myself experience when they first come here mainly comes from the fact that they are uneducated. If you are illiterate you have less confidence in yourself and don't like to venture out alone at first. You know that you will not be able to understand one word of what people say or be able to make yourself understood to them, so what is the use of going? Then after a while you pick up a few words here and there, you get bored staying in all the time and you pluck up courage. So when someone says they are going out you say, 'I think I should like to go out too, let me come with you.' Then they show you what to do and soon you are able to go alone any time you please.

Now of course I don't need anyone, I know how to do everything for myself. My husband often does come shopping with us on Saturday if he is free, but I am quite capable of doing it alone if necessary. Of course shopping is made simpler for people like us over here because in England the prices are all written on the goods telling you how much this costs, how much that costs, and so you don't have to ask anyone. And the prices are fixed in each shop so that you don't have to bargain either. I soon learnt to find out where the cheap stores were before setting out. All the same, I did not think much of the food which I saw on sale here. Nothing is fresh, all the vegetables look as though they have been left to wither for eight days, and even then they are dear at the price. In our village we could pick our vegetables fresh from the fields and in Delhi everything was brought in fresh each day also. Over there we wouldn't think of bringing home anything that was not perfectly sound and fresh. If the spinach looked stale or crushed, if the fruit was not properly ripened or the greens were not a nice fresh colour, we would say, 'Don't let us take those, they are no good.' Here you can't afford to be so particular; in England, however second rate the vegetables look, we say, 'Never mind, once we have cooked them they won't taste too bad.' For in any other shop they will be just the same. Here you have to eat stuff that would be thrown to the buffaloes in India.

Almost from the very start I went out to work. I only stayed sitting around at home for about six weeks after my arrival, for in the second month I got a job in the factory where my husband was working. I used to travel three miles each day. At about the same time we arranged for the children to attend school. A woman who came from the same village as myself in India had been visiting us one day when she remarked, 'Isn't it time you sent the children to school?' This reminded my husband and he made all the necessary inquiries and whatnot. Soon Sarinder and Asha were settled in their schools nearby.

Pritam did not go because she was sick at the time. All of them were unwell a lot of the time during the first six months what with fevers and coughs and colds. But Pritam's health was our main worry. When they asked him why our elder daughter was not at school my husband explained that she was sick and could not attend and they said she should be sent to hospital. She had become really bad and must have stayed at least two months in hospital. I shall not forget that time in a hurry. I was at work by then and when I came out in the evening I would go straight to the hospital from the factory. It meant crossing half London on my own but I could not neglect my poor daughter. I would not leave the hospital until I had seen her have her supper and settled down to sleep. Only then would I come home and make a meal for the others. It would be about seven or eight o'clock by that time, and there would be just enough time to eat and fall into bed if we were to get enough sleep to be up at seven the next morning. Right from the start our life here was not easy and we had many worries.

Chapter 55

GOING TO WORK

WHEN I started work it was my husband's idea that I should take a job, not my own. He had written to me while I was still in India that in London many women go out to work and that it is easy for them to find employment. If we both worked, he said, we could earn good money between us and afford to live really comfortably. I was quite willing to try, and besides, once I arrived in England I quickly saw for myself that the best thing for us would be to save up and buy our own house here, as soon as possible.

So my husband went to his manager and told him that he wanted to find a job for his wife. The manager said, 'Why don't you give her a little time to settle down in this country. Wait a few weeks and then we can find a place for her here.' So within two months of my arrival I was out to work. I worked in the same factory as my husband and I have been working there for most of the time since, although he later changed his job and now works somewhere else.

At first I used to work from nine in the morning until four in the afternoon, and I earned only seven pounds. I couldn't work full-time you see – let alone overtime – because Asha was only little and I had to collect her from school each day. I did not like having to work at first because we were living in one place and the factory was at another, and it was a long way to go from the factory to the school. I had to leave the house at eight in the morning each day in order to get to work on time, and then it was a rush in the afternoon to get back in time to collect Asha and give the children their evening meal. Now it is a little easier for me in this respect because we have bought a house which is not far from our work, but it is still very different from the leisurely life I used to lead in Delhi.

On the other hand, I never disliked the work itself at all. At first I was the only Indian amongst the women in the factory – since then I have helped several Indian women to get jobs there, and there are quite a lot of us working here. The people in the factory often ask me to bring along any friends of mine who need work, as there are plenty of jobs going for them. The work was very easy, just assembling and sorting. My husband was working in the room next door to mine. My chair was just beside the door so if I wanted to know something all I had to do was to run next door and ask him and then slip back to my chair. I did not know any English at that time, but there was seldom any difficulty. The work was so easy, there was nothing to explain. The charge-hand would just leave the articles to be assembled on my table, let me get on with the task, and then pick them up and take them away herself when I had finished them. What was there which needed explaining in that? The English people there liked me because I worked hard; it was all so simple that I could get through the work very quickly. And after all, hard work is what wins an English person's approval, isn't it? I could complete plenty of work for them in a day.

I liked the factory once I was used to it. In the room where I work now we are eight women. All the English women work downstairs, upstairs we are just four Jamaicans and four Indians. We eight work away happily up there on our own. Our charge-hand is a Jamaican woman, a nice person. We enjoy ourselves together, just getting on with our work and earning our pennies at our own pace. We have fun together because no one interferes with us; if the charge-hand is off sick we are just left to ourselves. Yes, mine is a very good job.

After only a few months I had to leave the factory because I was expecting my baby boy. But as soon as he was two months old I found a baby-minder near our house and went back to work again. At first I had thought I would get work in a laundry that was just near to where we lived, so one day I went there on my own and asked if there were any jobs available there. They told me that at present there were none but that if I would leave my name with them they might be able to employ me later. From the laundry I went to fetch Pritam from school and as I was walking along I thought to myself, 'Now why don't I go and ask at the same factory where I used to work?' The very next day I went along and they said, 'Yes, there is plenty of work. Start this very day if you like.' 'I can't start to-day,' I told them, 'but I will be along next week.' I never had any trouble finding work.

I got on well with all the people at work. I don't interfere with anyone's affairs and I keep myself to myself. Mind you, there have been some serious quarrels among the other women while I have been there. One Indian woman had a disagreement with another one day. She was rather the stronger of the two, so do you know what she did? She grabbed hold of the other and gave her a few good slaps on the face. Some time ago there was an even worse quarrel. One Indian woman had criticised another behind her back. Someone had reported this bit of backbiting to the victim of the gossip and she got really angry. 'Just let her come along and I will ask her straight out what she said about me,' she told everyone. We could see that real trouble was brewing up because this woman was a proper fighter. The English people there were not aware of what was going on at all, because of course they could not understand our language. But some of the Indian men who were working there overheard what was being said and the husbands of the two women began to abuse each other too. What an uproar was going on! The next day the two factions brought along all their children, friends, and relations with them, all ready for a real battle. They even started beating each other up outside the factory gates. Then the management had to telephone the police and ask them to take the culprits away. That was quite a fight – it started a court case which ran for I don't know how many months before they settled everything.

My job is a very good one and I am quite satisfied with it, but all the same I wish that it was not necessary for me to work, for the sake of my children. In India you spend your childhood playing in your mother's lap. Here we have to give our children to someone to look after and go out to work all day to get the money we need. A mother sees little of her children that way. In the morning I have to bundle the baby off to the baby-minder; there is no time to soothe him if he cries – only to stuff the bottle in his mouth, poor thing. Who knows whether the baby-minder looks after him properly all day long or not? I have no way of knowing. For all I know she may just shut him in the bedroom if he cries too much. All the time I am out at work I can't tell how my children have spent their day. I am not there to see whether they laugh or cry. And they know just as little of what I have been doing all day. In India mothers and children are together all the time – it is the husbands who earn the money. There every child gets his mother's milk to drink; I had to start giving Pappi a bottle at six weeks so that I could return to work.

I know that most English women who have children work part-time if they go out to work at all. But if we don't both work we can't save enough to do all we want to do. And if we can't live really well, what will have been the use of coming to this country in the first place? We were not so badly off in Delhi. First of all we were saving for the house and now we save in order to be able to go back to India for a visit. Now if I want to visit my parents I shall have four children to take with me, and even four half fares come to a great deal of money. And there is always a need of money for the house; the mortgage is to be paid, and there are repairs and decorations to be paid for as well. Now I earn about eleven pounds a week full-time, but I have to kill myself in order to do it. Once you are over here you are trapped, tied down by the very expense of living here, and it is difficult to escape.

Chapter 56

LEARNING ENGLISH

ONCE I had started work I did not find it too difficult to pick up a little English. All the English I know I have learnt in the factory, because that is almost the only place where I meet English people to speak to. You can't learn English just by sitting at home, can you? At first I didn't even know the difference between 'yes' and 'no'. Then when they said to me, 'Take this', 'Do this', 'This is your work', it was not hard for me to guess what the words meant and remember them. I soon started to understand simple instructions and the names of things.

I can make myself understood now and talk to English people a little, but I still can't say anything complicated. I can't explain any deep matter. Yet I think our Indian people learn English when they come here much more quickly than English people learn our language when they go to India. When white people come to Delhi they hardly ever bother to learn Punjabi or Hindi. Of course many people in India speak English whereas nobody here speaks Punjabi, so there is not the same pressing necessity for them to learn our language. But I still think that our Indian women settle down more quickly and are less helpless over here than the English women who go to India.

I watch the television programme on Sunday morning[1] and have learnt a little and I have had a few lessons from a friend. Now I can even read a few words in English and I know my ABC. I can read several pages of my reading book. Asha has helped me with my reading because she has learnt English at school. She tells me her teacher says she should practise her

1. Satya is referring to the B.B.C. programme for immigrants from India and Pakistan.

182

English more and play more with English children, but she seems to me to know plenty of words. But as I can't read her school reports I don't know exactly what her teacher means.

I first started to want to learn to read when someone told me that some of the tinned foods we buy at the supermarkets contain beef. We eat meat sometimes, but we don't eat beef because for us the cow is a pure and holy animal. I thought that if I could only recognise the word 'beef' when I saw it written I could avoid buying anything which contained it. Because they write on the outside of the tin what they have put into it, don't they? When I had learnt that 'beef' is B, double E, F, I thought, 'Why not learn a little more?' and I became interested in the idea of learning to read properly.

But I still feel that my lack of English makes it difficult for me. I have been here now for about five years but I am not satisfied with my English. If only I had more time I could sit down and memorise the words properly. Words like 'selfish' and 'hungry' are difficult for us to say and I need to practise them if I am to remember them. And I always find it hard to remember the difference between 'angry' and 'hungry'. You can't learn unless you practise but I am so busy earning money all day, and when I get back home I don't have a moment to myself away from the children to study quietly. In some houses there are several grown women, mother-in-law and daughter-in-law, or two sisters-in-law, and the work can be divided between them so that each has some time to herself, but in our household if anything is to be done I have to do it myself.

And for uneducated people like myself, who have never been to school, it is hard to start learning something later in life. I feel that I have passed the age when it is easy to pick up new things quickly. When I want to say anything it is the Punjabi words which I have already learnt that come most readily to my lips. If I had ever studied at school no doubt I should have formed the habit of memorising new words. All the same, I have always felt that I ought to make the effort to learn so as not to be completely helpless here, and I am sorry that I have not been able to achieve more.

Chapter 57

'NO TIME FOR AFFECTION'

AT first I did not know a soul in this country apart from the Indians who worked in the shop below our rooms. And when I started work first of all there were no other Indians besides ourselves in the factory. I used to feel so lonely that I wondered why we had ever come to this country. I could not speak English and there was no one with whom I could talk in Punjabi. There were a hundred little things which would come to my mind, but no friend to whom I could tell them in my own language.

But after a month or two, when another Indian woman started work in our factory, things got better. She was a Punjabi like me. And then a Sindhi woman joined us and I became quite friendly with her. Those two women lived near to our house and so we began visiting each other, we three people. Since then I have made quite a lot of friends at the factory. My special friends are two women who now work alongside me. I quite often go to the suburb where they live as there are many Indian shops there, and I call in at their houses when I can. They come to see me, too. They called in every day when I was in bed with 'flu not long ago; they used to come during the lunch hour and share the food they had brought for their lunch with me. And I went with them when the son of one of them was taken to hospital after he met with an accident. All of us went together. At first we could not find the right ward and wandered about not knowing what to do. But then I plucked up courage to ask a nurse and she explained to me where we could find the boy. I understood enough to find the way to the ward where he was lying.

The trouble in this country is that if you go out to work you never have time to do all the visiting you would like to do. To-day I had thought of going to see someone, but then I thought, 'No, to-morrow is Monday; if I go now I will never have time to get the children's clothes washed and ironed ready for school to-morrow.'

Plenty of people from my own village have come to England but I am not in contact with many of them. For one thing they are not all living in London; some are in Birmingham, others are in Leicester. And you must remember that it is getting on for twenty years since I married and left our village. In that time the people I remember as children have grown up and married – how do I know in whose household babies have been born, or how many children they have? Letters come from time to time telling us that so-and-so has gone to England but I can't always recall who so-and-so may be. We have made contact with a few, though. When we had only been here for a little under a year someone mentioned our arrival to a boy from our village who had been living near us for some time. He told them that he could not remember Satya but he did remember her elder sister. When we came to know that he was here, living so near to us, we decided to call on him, and he returned our call a little later. After a few visits like this we became very friendly and he said that he would like me to consider him as a brother. In India a woman who has no brothers or who is far from her own brothers can 'adopt' a boy she knows, to be her new brother. If they consent to become brother and sister to each other the boy must give her presents and look after her and her children, just like a real brother. Well, this 'brother' of mine has been very good to us; when Pappi was born he gave me several lengths of cloth for my own clothes as well as things for the baby. And recently he gave a new dress to each of my girls when we went to visit him. Very fine dresses they were – shiny cloth embroidered with silver thread.

So nowadays I do not feel so lonely as I did at first. There are few Indians living in the streets around our house, but we have so many Indian acquaintances not far off that I never lack company. But all the same, it is not like the society we knew in India because there we were surrounded by my own family.

Neither my husband nor I have our family here and I feel that my children are missing something because of this. In India a child is the darling of all his relatives. If he cries, it is just as likely to be one of his aunts or his grandmother who picks him up and comforts him as his own mother. He hardly knows whose baby he really is because so many people are around him, ready to give him anything he asks for. For my children there is no one who can take the place of the aunts and uncles they have left behind over there.

And over there, all the family are there to help you – and what a lot of relatives there are! If your mother's sister is not free to come and lend a hand when you need it, then your father's sister will be able to spare the time. If your father's mother is not around when you need help, then your mother's mother will manage to turn up. And people are more neighbourly too. If anything needs to be done you can usually call on a neighbour to help you. In this country you barely know who your neighbours are, let alone whether they are good folk or bad folk. I don't even have a moment to catch a glimpse of our neighbours' faces in the morning, because it is time to skip along to the factory at eight o'clock. And when we get in at night we feel too tired to stand around chatting with anyone. We just have time to make our supper and roll up in the bedclothes. You only get acquainted with your neighbours if you are at home all day; then you see each other coming and going and get to know each other. Or if you have time to lounge outside or take a stroll in the evening, you meet them and chat together. But who has time to lounge outside in this country? Even if the weather is good, the only chance I have to spend a little time in the garden is when I hang the washing out on Sunday.

If I say this over and over again it is because it is what I feel most deeply about this country – that here there is no room for affection in people's lives. This is true both of the English and of the Indians who come to live here – the Indians become like the English because they are working under the same conditions. Here no one takes thought for the other. In India, if I hear that someone is ill I set off that very second to find out how they are, to see if they want anything or if there is anything I can do. If the milk happens to be on the fire at that moment – never mind, let it boil over, but go I must. And never mind whether it is my mother who needs me, my sister or a friend, I will go over there and then out of my affection for them. It is our custom and it is only right; how can it feel to lie sick on your bed all day watching the door and wondering if anyone will come to see you? A sick person can't get up and remind others of his existence, he can only lie and fret if everyone seems to have forgotten him. But if someone comes to visit him he will forget his pain for a while. In India we go to visit a sick person the minute we come to know of their illness, but here a man might die waiting for someone to come to his house and inquire after him.

I am not saying that I am better than anyone else in this respect. I myself cannot find time to visit people as much as I should. If I hear that someone is ill, even if it is only Monday when the news arrives, I have to say, 'I had better leave it until Sunday to visit them if I am to go at all.' People who arrive from our village or people that we know here are always giving us their addresses, telling us, 'Come over and see us when you can.' They complain loudly if we don't go, but the weekend is so short. I don't finish work until 12.30 on Saturday. Only last week someone invited us to a *path* held to celebrate the birth of their son. It was to last three days and every day we kept on saying, 'To-morrow we will go,' but in the end we never found time. In India we would go as a matter of duty, just like that. People are too busy making money for themselves over here to find time to love each other. If you are after money then this country is a fine place, but if you are looking for affection, then there is much more of it to be found in India.

Chapter 58

A NEW BABY

I WAS very happy when I came to know that I was expecting another baby. Some Indian people say that babies born over here are more intelligent than those born in India and our Pappi is certainly a very clever baby. The day before he was born I had to go to the hospital for a check up – I used to go every Wednesday. There wasn't anything wrong with me that Wednesday, but I went to the hospital all the same as usual after giving everybody their breakfast. When I got there they told me that it looked as though the baby would arrive very soon and that the moment I could feel anything I should telephone for the ambulance. Then the ambulance would bring me straight to the hospital. I explained to them that there was no telephone in my house and that my husband was doing night shifts and so might not be there to fetch the ambulance for me. I told a lie because he was not on night shifts at all, but I thought that they might admit me there and then if I told them that, and so save a lot of bother. Sure enough, they asked me, 'Would you like to stay here then?' I said, 'Yes, I have no telephone, no car, and my husband will be at work to-night. I will come in to-day.' I went home to fetch my nighties and everything, and set off for the hospital again in the bus alone. I did not need anyone with me, and so the idea never entered my head to ask my husband to accompany me. I thought, 'When the others come home they will guess where I have gone.' I got to the hospital in the afternoon and they put me to bed. I just lay there quietly and comfortably. It was summer-time and the evenings were light and long. Someone said to me, 'Hasn't your husband come to see you?' but really it hadn't occurred to me to wonder whether anyone would come or not. I had thought, 'My husband must have arrived home by now; he must be cooking for the children at this moment, since I am not there to prepare a meal for them.'

They gave me a bath, then I had an injection, and when I was in bed again they brought me a meal. I felt very comfortable and just went on lying restfully. I did not feel at all anxious or afraid; I knew that it was all in the hands of God whether I should be delivered easily or not. Then early the next morning I began to feel the pains starting, but I just went on resting quietly until they became very strong. Then I called the nurse and said, 'I have some pains now.' She took me away to the room where they deliver the babies.

I am told that it is the fashion for English women to have their husbands with them when they are in labour but to me this idea seems ridiculous. What is the husband supposed to be doing – is it he who is giving birth, or the woman? I may be an illiterate woman but when there is a job to be done I just get on and do it on my own. I have a strong heart and I am not like some women who make a fuss and cry 'Booh-hooh' if there is the slightest thing the matter with them. If I am in labour you can bring my nearest and dearest into the room and it would make no difference to me. While I was having a pain I would probably say, 'Clear all these people out of here and let me get on with it!' When the labour was finished then I should be ready to smile at everyone even if you sat ten people down round my bed.

Pappi was born very soon after they took me to the delivery room. At that very moment the nurse asked me, 'How many children have you got?' and I answered, 'Three – or rather four counting this one.' Then she asked, 'Are they boys or girls.' 'Two girls and one boy,' I said. 'Well,' she said, 'now you have got one boy more.' I was very pleased and excited. Just then someone came in to say that my husband had arrived and was waiting outside. He had gone to work that morning and told the people that his wife had gone into hospital the night before. They said to him, 'Then what did you want to come to work for, thick-head? What are you doing here if your wife is in hospital. Aren't you going to go and find out how she is getting on? Who knows what might have happened in the night?' So he got leave to take the morning off and arrived at the hospital at half-past-ten, hardly half an hour after Pappi was born. The nurse said to me, 'Would you like to see your husband now? I have told him about the baby and he is very happy.' Of course I said, 'Yes, let him come in.' She let him in and brought us a pot of tea. Then she said to him, 'Now pour your wife a nice cup of tea.' 'What is the matter?' I said, 'There is nothing wrong with me that I can't pour it myself. Just pass me the cups over here.' So I poured out tea for us both. After that my husband went off to tell everyone that we had got a son, he was so excited.

Chapter 59

HUSBANDS AND WIVES

I STAYED in hospital for eleven days and he would usually come in the evening to see me and the new baby. Once he brought the children with him too. I used to watch the English women in the ward and wonder at them. There was one woman in the bed opposite mine who used to make such a to-do if her husband did not come every night to see her. She would cry and cry and complain to everyone that her husband had not come to see her. 'What a dreadful thing,' I thought. 'Isn't she ashamed to carry on like that in front of everyone?' If my husband ever missed an evening I never bothered. I had nothing to complain of, after all; lying there contentedly I would think, 'There is nothing for me to grumble about here; people have sent me so many flowers, the nurses do everything for the baby, they bring me my food, and I have nothing to do but rest and enjoy myself.' I knew that if my husband didn't turn up it must be because he was either too tired after a long day's work or because he was busy looking after the children.

Another thing that I noticed is that English women do not show very much modesty in front of men. If anyone came to see me in the evening in hospital I would put on a *kamiz* over my nightie. I had a long-sleeved *kamiz* with me, and even though I was lying in bed I would pull it on if anyone came or else throw a shawl round my shoulders. I should feel ashamed if any man but my husband were to see me half-dressed like that but the other women there didn't seem to mind. One day my husband brought an Indian neighbour of ours along with her husband. I made him laugh. I said, 'Brother, doesn't this place look just like the sea-side?' He, poor man, was sitting huddled up by his wife, trying to keep his back turned to all those other women, he felt so embarrassed. 'Is this a hospital,' I said, 'or is it the sea-side?' He had to laugh. But he didn't stay long, he felt so awkward. He only sat a little while and then he said to his wife, 'Come along, Darshana, I think it is time we were moving now.'

I was shocked by the way couples in this country kiss in public too. In the hospital all the husbands who came used to kiss their wives right there in front of everyone. I didn't like it at all, to me it seemed very bad. I don't think my husband is any less affectionate than anyone else's but he and I have other ways of showing our affection for each other. For instance, in the hospital he would come and sit down by my bed and then he would ask me gently what sort of day I had had; whether the baby had taken his milk all right; had he cried at all? And I would ask him what he had done all day, what time he had got back from work, what he had cooked for the children. Then he would say, 'I will just go and have a look at our baby.' We can express our affection just as well in this way and show that we care about each other. We never feel the need to kiss in public or hold hands for everyone to see. After all, love is in the heart, isn't it, not in the hands? You don't have to walk along locked in each other's arms all the time to show that you love each other. In any case I don't think that a woman ingratiates herself to her husband by doing this sort of thing. Once a relationship is established between them, it is established. If the man likes his wife he will stay with her, and if he doesn't he won't. He will not love her the more if she makes a fuss.

I have heard it said that English people think that Indian women are dominated by their husbands, but I think that this is rubbish. I think that the real difference between Indian and English marriages is that we Indian women are less dependent on our husbands for company and affection. In England it is the husband alone who takes the responsibility for the woman after she is married. In India the responsibility is divided among so many people. Even when she is married, the burden of her welfare is still on her parents' head. Suppose I am in India and I have to go to hospital; my mother will come to see how I am, my sisters-in-law will come, my brothers and sisters, my mother-in-law – the whole family. If my husband does not manage to come it won't make much difference to me. I shall hardly notice, because there will be so many other people round me. Anyway he can always excuse himself by saying, 'I didn't like to come while your mother and sisters were with you because I felt shy about meeting them.'

Chapter 60

MODERN MARRIAGES

I HAVE already told you, and what I have seen in England makes me the more convinced, that our Indian marriages are very firmly based. Over here the couple go to church and the girl's mother says, 'There, now our daughter is off our hands.' Even if the boy leaves her after a couple of weeks, people will say, 'All right, she can get a divorce; she will find another man;

It is up to her.' The parents don't think she is their responsibility any more.

Even amongst our Indian people many boys nowadays like to take a look at the girls their parents have chosen for them. They like to find out whether the bride is good-looking or not. And there are even love marriages amongst Indians too, both here and in India. The boys and girls study together in schools and colleges. They meet there and arrange things among themselves. The boy will say to his father, 'I like that girl. I want to marry her,' and if his parents are agreeable then things go ahead and a dowry of some kind will be given. Often, though, they disapprove of their son's choice. They are angry and say, 'All right, if you insist on doing things your own way, you can clear out of our house.'

But the trouble with love marriages is that until you live with a person you can only find out the superficial things about him. Many people make bad mistakes in this way. Some people even break their caste to marry someone they have taken a fancy to. For example, we knew of a Chamar boy – a neighbour of ours here in London – who had come over here to study. (Chamars are a very low caste in India.) When he went back to India he met a Khatri girl and they wanted to marry each other because they had fallen in love. They got married and returned here together to set up house. It was only then that the girl discovered that her husband was of a very low caste. He had tried to keep the fact concealed, but somehow everyone came to know of it. How that poor girl must have regretted what she had done when she found out. I have met that girl myself – her baby daughter was born only a few weeks back. Everyone here says how sickly she is looking these days. It is no wonder when you think how troubled she must feel.

All the same, most Indians over here don't have love marriages. They get married in the usual way. The only difference is that they don't worry quite so much about what sort of wage the boy is earning when they choose a groom, because over here, if the worst comes to the worst, the woman can always work to get her bread. In India it is difficult for women to get work. And over here they give bigger dowries because they earn more money. In India they start to gather things together for their daughter's dowry when she is so high, but here they know that a few months' wages will take care of the whole thing. At one wedding I went to – just lately it was – the girl's parents had got one ring made for the groom, another for his mother and a third for his uncle. They were all made of eight *tollas* of gold, ear-rings of two *tollas* each and four bangles of two *tollas* each. There were outfits of clothing for all the boy's relatives, a big tape-recorder, and a complete set of furniture. Some people over here prefer to give cash – two hundred or four hundred pounds – or as much as they can afford. But whichever way they do it they always give something. Some Pakistani people we knew of gave their girl a house. Her father was dead and her other brothers and sisters all married so her mother transferred the house to her name as a dowry along with – I don't know how much – about Rs. 15,000 cash.

English people get married with only one ring. Just one ring! Well, I suppose that is all right. If no one expects gifts then no one will grumble afterwards that they weren't given this, that, or the other. If there is no giving and receiving, then it certainly saves expense. He says he loves her and she says she loves him and that is that. But I can see now that if our Indian marriages are more elaborate and expensive they hardly ever end in divorce. They are altogether tougher and do not break so easily.

Chapter 61

BEING COLOURED (2)

I CANNOT say that I have ever been the victim of colour prejudice myself. I know that there are English people who do not like Indians to live in their houses but we have always rented rooms from other Indians. And I know that English people don't like their daughters to marry Indians. I have heard of many Indian boys who have married English girls in London and it seems that the girl's parents are seldom pleased. But no one has ever said anything to me personally. Sometimes English people talk about it in the factory, but not to me; that sort of talk has never got in the way of my work and I have heard colour talked about more on the television than amongst the people I know.

But of course I don't know many English people and my English is poor. As I don't always understand what they say I can't always be sure of what English people mean when they talk to me. The lady who used to look after Pappi at first – she was white. Later I changed to another baby-minder but she asked me several times when we met in the street, 'Why don't you leave Pappi with me again?' She would laugh when she said it. Now, I could not tell whether she said it as a joke, or whether she said it because she was in need of money, or because she was fond of the baby. It is difficult to tell people's intentions. But still, no one ever said to me, 'You are coloured, we don't like to take coloured babies.' And if I go shopping no one has ever refused to serve me, and neither of us has ever been refused a job because we are Indian, so far.

On the Sunday television programme for Indians, they never interview an English person and ask him what he thinks. Why don't they invite some ordinary sensible English person who knows a little of our language (or they could translate for him) and then we could really know what English people think? They could ask him, 'What do you think about coloured people?' and he would tell us. After all, it is a matter for the people whose country it is to decide. But they only invite Indians or big people on that programme, so we don't know what the English public is really thinking.

But if the English people don't like Indians, in my opinion it is their own folly that they let them into their country. No Indian can come here except through the English government. He gets his voucher through the government; it is a government official who stamps his passport at the airport; if his children are born here or if he marries, it is the government which issues the certificate. Without the government's good will we people can do nothing. The government is like mother and father to us Indians here and so it is in their hands to let us in or keep us out. It is their fault if too many coloured people are here, not ours. Look, if one of our children tells tales or misbehaves, won't people complain to us first of all, because we are his parents? What he does is our responsibility. And just as the child looks up to his parents to tell him what to do and what not to do, so we look to the government because we can only do things through them. Our relationship is with the English government rather than with English people. It is for the government to decide whether to allow us in or not.

If the government lets coloured people in when English people are against it, it is their own foolishness. Except for a few, the Indians who come here don't creep into the country like thieves, they don't cheat to get here; they come because the government invites them by giving them a voucher. And those who get in by false pretences, for instance by claiming that they have only come for a visit or that they have only come in order to get married to someone living here – they could be stopped at entry if they were more strict at the airport. Once a man has got out of the airport it is difficult to catch him. Anyway, the government could always refuse to issue marriage certificates to such people. They could say, 'No, brother, I am afraid you can't get married here; you must go back to your own country,' and that would be that. If they did that, it would nip race troubles in the bud.

If English people don't like us, they are only bewailing their own follies. They could have stopped the government from letting us come. If they are not prepared to do that then they are only cutting off their nose to spite their face. But I don't think that they should turn out those who are already fully settled here. Those who come alone – single men and women – what does it matter to them where they live? They have few ties. But those who have brought their families over here, made their homes here, perhaps sold up all their land in India and whose whole life is in this country – it would be wrong to send them back. What would they do back in India anyway? If they are beaten out of this country you can be sure that they would only make a nuisance of themselves over there. But in the end it is up to English people to decide, and they should think very carefully about this matter.

Chapter 62

'A GREAT SIN'

ONCE we had settled in here the next decision which we had to make was whether to invite my husband's father over to join us. Before we had left India we had told him that we would always send him money, and so we did. We never wanted him to feel resentful or say, 'They went off and deserted me.' We did not fear that he would not be properly looked after; in India some neighbour will always tend a sick person or bring water to an invalid who finds himself alone, and anyway my brother-in-law had agreed that the old man should live with him. But we did not want anyone to feel bitter about the matter or to say after we had gone, 'That is all very fine for you –

running off to England to earn money while we are left to care for your old man.' Even though we sent plenty of money people might have gossiped and we did not want them to say, 'They left the poor old fellow to starve.' People notice things and we did not want to feel any cause for shame in front of them.

But I soon came to realise from what I saw of the condition of elderly Indians brought to this country that we would certainly have been doing wrong to bring my father-in-law over here. I have seen it happen over and over again and it is people's own fault; the old people get their son's letter from England telling them of his prosperity and their hearts begin to blacken. 'They are having a fine time over there,' they think, 'they are not sparing a thought for us left behind in India.' (Fine time indeed – they don't know how hard you have to work over here to earn your fine time.) Or they feel discontented that their sons do not write to them more often – as though anyone over here had time to sit down and write to India every day. So the son brings his old mother or father here, and at first they are delighted. 'Now we shall be with our son at last,' they think as they step into the plane. 'Everything will be all right; every day they will give us meat to eat, even wine if we want it. We shall pass our old age in ease and luxury.' And suppose an old man arrives on a Saturday, everything is all right for the first day; and on Sunday he likes England very much also. But when the son has to run to his work and the daughter-in-law to her factory! They know that the old man may not know how to use the gas stove or the geyser and the other appliances which we use over here, and they know that it may be dangerous for him; if he were to turn on the gas and forget to light it he might be dead before anyone arrived home and found out. So they leave some food already prepared or pack something in a Thermos flask. And when the poor old fellow has to eat stale food at mid-day he begins to think, 'I was all right where I was in India. At least over there I got food fresh and hot from the stove. Did I come so many miles just to eat stale bread?' And when the young people come in from school or work they are tired out. 'Make us a cup of tea,' says the old man as soon as his daughter-in-law appears, or, 'What about some nice hot vegetables now?' But she is so tired and stiff from standing and running around all day that she can't jump up that very minute to fulfil his demands. So the old man gets angry and peevish – because in India the young people wait on their elders and respect their every wish. 'She didn't even ask if I felt hungry,' he says to himself. 'All very well calling me "father-in-law" and then not even making me a cup of tea when I need it!'

The old people get bored and lonely over here, too. It is hard enough for us to learn a new language and adjust to new ways, but they are past the age when they can adapt easily. If they want company while the others are out all day, or if they want to know something, whom can they go and ask? An old person here is as helpless as a child and must rely on someone else coming to tell him. He cannot understand the people around him, nor can they understand him. I can get a baby-minder for my baby, but where could I leave my poor old father-in-law?

It is not so bad for those families who live in areas where there are already many Indians settled. There an old man can go to the park on a fine day and meet other old Indian men. They can all sit on a bench together and have a good chat – gossip about their grandchildren, boast about their sons, grumble about their daughters-in-law to their heart's content. 'Lentils she gave us yesterday – but they were all dried up and sticking to the pan.' It is just like when people take their dogs for exercise in the park; they let their dog loose and he meets another dog; the dogs meet together and enjoy themselves and then they don't give any trouble to their owners.

But not everyone lives in such circumstances. The old man gets bored and discontented and the best thing for him would be to spend a few months at a time with each of his children. He will probably want this himself, as this is how old people frequently spend their time in India. But it is costly enough to get to England in the first place – who can afford to take a trip to India once a year, what with a mortgage, rates, electricity and I don't know what other expenses to save for?

I have seen this pattern of events with my own eyes as well as hearing about it from the Indians we know in this country. English people think that all Indians are only waiting for the day when they can bring their elderly dependents over here and that the old people themselves are just as delighted to be here, but usually it is quite another story, and they are less contented here than they would be in India.

So we decided not to ask my father-in-law to come and join us. If we had had so much money that I could stay at home all day and attend to him it would have been a different matter. But it is bad enough that I have to abandon my baby to some-one else's care all day, without creating more problems. My father-in-law stayed with my husband's younger brother in Delhi until he died not long ago and I think that he was quite happy.

Plenty of people in our position would encourage their brothers or brothers-in-law to come over here too but we have been through so many difficulties, why should we drag others into trouble too? They would want to bring their wives and children along also, and it would not be much easier for them than it has been for us. Now we are on the way to seeing an end to the difficult times we have been through, but it is hard to know what to say in our letters home. If we grumble that life is hard here they will say, 'What is keeping you in England then?' But if we say what a splendid time we are having here they will say at home, 'Why do you want to keep it all to your-selves? Why not let us join you?' Actually my brothers do not ask us to help them to come here; they know that it is getting more difficult to come here these days. Our Rampal says that if any of our relatives should come of his own accord by getting himself a voucher then we shall do everything we can to assist him; but we should not encourage anyone to leave a good job in India only to live in misery over here. I myself also think that it would be a great sin and that is the truth.

Chapter 63

'STANDING ON THEIR OWN TWO FEET'

Now that I have told you of all the difficulties which we have had to face since coming here you may feel like asking 'Well, why don't you go back home to India if you find life so hard here?' Indeed sometimes I have asked myself the same thing. But the trouble is that once a man comes over here he is stuck. If we were to return, my husband would never find such a good job as the one he left to come here. And a family of three or four children like ours needs several hundred pounds for the fares alone.

Here everything costs so much that it is hard to save. We earn a decent wage each but after all that hard work every week it seems that the money is in our pockets on Friday and gone by Saturday. Some goes on the mortgage, some on the children's school dinners, some on food for the family – I hardly know where it all goes, but it takes most of the money we earn between us to maintain a standard of living that makes it worth our staying here. You would think that if a man brings home plenty of pennies each week he would be happy enough, but things are so dear over here that he ties his heart in knots with worry. On the other hand, every day he receives letters from India which tell him how low wages are over there and remind him of the sort of life he has just escaped from.

All the same, I hope we shall not stay here for ever. I envisage us putting up with it all for another fifteen, twenty years and then quietly going off home. It is true that we are not at all badly off here. The children are happy and we do not lack for anything we really need. But I sometimes feel afraid that there is not much security for us here. We depend on our jobs, which we had no difficulty in finding, but suppose we were unemployed? For myself, I would be only too pleased to be spending my time at home looking after the children and scrubbing the house, but you don't earn money that way, do you? And then there is this to think of – political conditions from what I hear are not very favourable to our Indian and Pakistani people. That is another source of worry. After establishing a home here we don't want to find ourselves turned out without warning, just like that.

You never know what may happen to you in the future, and that is why I believe in saving. My husband sometimes says he disagrees with me. We have been thinking of the future all our life, he says, why not enjoy the present a little? Certainly I don't think you should stint yourself of the things you need. You should eat nice food and wear decent clothes, but I don't believe you should squander the whole week's pay either. But we don't quarrel over it. He has no extravagant tastes like some men have, and so we are able to put by a little each month.

Not all Indians do as we do, of course. Some get intoxicated by the high wages they get and squander all they earn. I'll tell you about one boy we knew. He ate up all the money he had earned over here, even though his parents were always advising him to save. The silly fool did not use his brain. His father would write to him, 'Make a bit of money over there and save it up, then we shall be able to arrange a fine match for you when you come back. After all you are a grown man now and it is time that you got married.' So after a while he himself felt that it was time he had a wife and he went off back to India. His mother and father thought to themselves, 'Surely he will have brought some money for the wedding expenses. I expect he will give it to us in a few days' time.' But the days went by and no money was forthcoming. His parents thought, 'Surely he will give us the money in his own good time.' A whole month went by, his mother and father observing him closely so as to try to guess his intentions, and then at last his father said to him one day, 'Look, son, people earn fabulous sums of money in England. Now tell us the truth – how much have you brought home? Let us know so that we can make the arrangements for your wedding accordingly.' The silly boy felt very foolish and could not bring himself to reply. His father was perplexed and said, 'Come, put your hand on this cow's tail and tell us truthfully how much you were really earning in London.' (In our country if a person swears on the tail of a cow then he must tell the truth since the cow is a sacred animal; you see how different our customs are in India.) So the boy held the cow's tail and said, 'Father, the truth is that I really did earn plenty, but I consumed every penny of it; now arrange my marriage or not, it is up to you.' Actually they did get him married in the end because though he had brought no money with him, a man who returns from England is so much looked up to in India that you would not believe it. He gets so much respect and everyone would like him for a son-in-law.

But I don't approve of such people who cannot stand on their own two feet. Some people who come here are very helpless. A man called here the other day for instance, to ask our advice. He had lost his job and was unable to find another. Mind you he had only applied to one factory so I think it was a matter of not wanting to find one. Now, he told us, the Social Security people won't give him any more unemployment benefit, but they say that they would if he had his wife and children over here with him. His idea is that he should get married to a white woman he knows over here; then he will be able to say that he has a wife and they will give him some money. He is all very manly when it comes to marriage but not when it comes to hard work. We told him that he was being foolish. If he cannot support himself, how will he support a wife? And suppose the police find out that he already has a wife in India, won't they put him in jail? No, he said, they couldn't put him in jail because he had a British passport. I ask you – are there no English people inside jails here, or are they only full of Indians? Why can't that man do as my husband did – work hard and save a little at a time until his wife and children can come over too? Then she can go to work also and after a while they will establish themselves and have no difficulty. But if you won't lift a finger to help yourselves, then you can expect nothing.

We ourselves have always supported ourselves through our own efforts, and now we are gradually getting all the things we need. We started looking for a house as soon as we had enough money for the deposit, about two years ago. We went to an estate agent, but we did not like the houses he showed us at first at all. One house belonged to some Pakistanis, but it had no fence between the front garden and the road. Leave your door just a few inches ajar and anybody's dogs and cats could get inside from the street. I told my husband, 'I don't like this house. Let us look for one with a better garden, where our children can play safely.' Then we saw some better houses, but they were all too expensive. After all, we were not sure that we would be able to get a mortgage easily, for many say that coloured people are not given mortgages readily, or at least can only get them at high rates of interest. When we saw this house I told the agent that it suited us well but it was too expensive. I asked whether the price could be reduced a little. 'Look these people are not babies, that they can be fooled into dropping £700,' he said, 'but we can certainly try. Please yourself.' So we went to see the owners ourselves. Only the owner's wife was at home, and we had to bargain with her in broken English because we did not know very much English at that time. We eventually managed to make ourselves understood and she agreed to lower the price somewhat. We accomplished this without any help from others, so cannot other people do the same?

We have decorated the two downstairs rooms in our house now that the better weather has come; the front room has beautiful shiny paper and gold coloured curtains to match, and the back room has flowered paper and a new carpet. We did all the work ourselves at the weekends. And my husband laid new lino in the kitchen and fixed strip lighting there. What I should really like now is a proper bathroom; our bathroom is downstairs and has not got a decent wash basin. I have heard that you can get a grant for your bathroom, but you would have to pay the money back, wouldn't you? And we can't afford that on top of the mortgage just now. A few weeks ago my husband bought this refrigerator second hand for a few pounds, along with some other good second hand furniture, from a friend of his. And I have ordered a pair of gold earrings from an Indian goldsmith – the latest design from India. They cost about twenty pounds, gold being cheaper here than it is in India.

Except for the house itself, of course, everything we have bought we have paid for in cash. I dare say some people's houses have nicer carpets than ours and they run big smart cars, but you'll often find that they have hardly a penny left to themselves each month by the time they have paid all the hire purchase instalments they owe for these fine things. I don't believe in running up debts – I have seen the trouble it leads to – and if we have the good things we want it is because we are as careful with our pennies over here as we used to be when we were in India.

Chapter 64

'SOMETIMES I AM VERY HAPPY, SOMETIMES VERY SAD'

I THINK that we encountered more difficulties in settling here than many of the Indians who arrive in England nowadays. Those who come these days usually have some relative or other, a friend, or at least someone of their own waiting for them over here. Many people have their entire family here. A person who already has close friends or relatives in this country has less trouble in finding his feet. They will visit him at his house to keep him company, they will help him to find a job, they will show him around, teach him what to do and what not to do. Gradually he learns from them how to manage. Suppose either of my brothers, or my husband's brother, or any relative of ours were to come to this country now – they would not face the same problems as ourselves because we would be here to help them. What trouble would they have? The biggest hardship is when you have to struggle alone in a strange country with no one to call your own.

We came several years ago when there were not so many Indians living in these parts. As we did not have any relative of our own to help us we had to rely on other people to show us what to do. And the more you rely on others to help you, the harder it is for affection to flourish between you. Suppose I am friends with you and I am always asking you to do things for me. Once, twice, three times you will help me willingly. But after that you will start to feel that I only want to be your friend for what I can get out of you. When you see me coming you will think, 'Here comes Satya, what can she be wanting now?' Then if you do what I ask you will be doing it resentfully, and if you refuse I will feel resentful and will think, 'You refused me on purpose because you did not want to help me.' Or suppose a sister whenever she visits her brother says, 'Give me this, brother, I have a right to it; give me that, brother, it is your duty to give it.' Then her brother will no longer look forward to her visits and his wife will complain that she has a grasping sister-in-law. But if she is able to say to her brother, even when he offers her help, 'No, brother, please don't worry about me. I have a family, but so have you. Do not deprive yourself and your children for my sake,' then won't her brother love her the more and won't his wife say, 'I have a very good sister-in-law, she never pesters us for anything'?

That is why our relationships with the Indian people we know over here have never been so close and warm as those we had with our friends and neighbours in India. Over there people help each other and ask each other into their houses willingly because no one depends entirely on the others. Here people are obliged to ask each other for help all the time – in finding a job, filling in forms and so on – and this creates resentment between them. So often people have expressed affection and said sweet words to us only to let us down afterwards. You can ask my husband how many times this has happened to us. We have done a lot for other people and we have had to ask other people to do things for us but love cannot survive where such demands are continual. If I have affection for someone I do not like to spoil that affection by asking for things. I can never feel that our friendships over here are as warm as those we knew in India. It is twenty years or so since I left my parents' house, and since then I have seen life a bit. In Delhi we mixed with all kinds of people – refugees from Pakistan, men and women from other parts of India – but during that time I never felt that my life lacked affection until I came over here.

Sometimes I feel very happy in this country, sometimes very sad. But at least so far as my children are concerned I do not have any real worries. If we stay here they will all be educated and have a good future. I don't know about Sarinder, he doesn't seem to like studying very much, but he may yet do well for himself if he works harder. And Pappi is very intelligent. Once he gets inside a school he will learn very fast, of that I am sure. I should like him to start school as early as possible, perhaps in another year's time, though I am not sure if they take three-year-old children in nursery schools here. He is almost two now but he knows how to say lots of things already, both in Punjabi and in English. He learns English from the woman who looks after him while I am at work and from his brothers and sisters. The other day they were showing a programme about Bradford on the television. He ran up and pointed to the television, and said, 'Look, Daddy, look at Bradford.' Everything you say to him, he will remember.

As for the girls, we shall get them married here. If we can't find suitable Indian boys for them here then we can send them to India to be married. But it should not be too hard to find good husbands for them in this country. Indian girls in England can pick and choose their husbands; how many unmarried Indian girls do you see around here for every unmarried Indian boy? Not many unmarried girls come here except those that come here with their parents, but young men are arriving here alone all the time, either to work or to study. When they settle here they start looking round for a wife and there are not so many girls here for them to choose from. Some get their wives from India, but for the Indian girl who lives here there are excellent chances of getting a husband with a good job, a house and money.

Of course I don't know yet what the children will want for themselves, when they grow up. I hope they will want the same things as we do. But at any rate when the time comes for them to get married they will know that we are ready to arrange everything for them. It would be nice if our sons stayed with us after they were married. Then we could help them if they were ever in trouble. They would have their own children and we would look after them and do all we could for them. Or if they didn't want to stay with us we would say, 'All right, once you are earning you set up your own homes and live where you like. You can come to visit us regularly and we will visit you.'

Nor have I any worries about my family in India. All my brothers and sisters are married and happily settled. Each is well provided for in his or her own home. None of them is very rich, but none of them is very poor either, just medium. My elder sister lives in Jalandhar. The sister who is next youngest to myself, the one who is married to my husband's younger brother, lives in Delhi. Her husband is employed by the Central Secretariat as a driver. They have four little girls now. Our next youngest sister lives in Pagvara where her husband is a labourer in a clothmill. They are not so well off as the others as he does not earn much, but they manage quite well. Then our youngest sister of all only got married about six months before I came to England. When I left she had not yet gone to live with her husband permanently. But now she is with him in Bangeshehr where he has his own business.

As for my brothers, the elder is still living in Delhi. He has two sons and a daughter. One son is with him in Delhi – he is only a couple of years younger than our Asha – but the elder son lives with my parents in the village, staying with them to help my father. My younger brother was married only a year or two ago and has no children as yet. He is a lathe worker at Guraen. All of us live in the towns now, you see. By all accounts every one of us has been fortunate and God has favoured us, for we are all happy in our homes.

I have no fears for my mother and father either. We send money to them and they are quite comfortably off. As long as we are sitting in England earning good money, and my brothers and sisters are over there in the Punjab, they will never need worry for money. My father has never had to sweat to earn his bread so far and we are not going to tell him, 'Run along and work for your living,' now that he is no longer young, as people do over here. My father has no anxieties now since all his children are married. He just gets on with his own business and my nephew is there to help him. He is free to please himself; sometimes he spends a few months here and there with his sons. He can come and go as he likes because he is still quite fit and active. He never asks us for anything and he has never complained that we do not return to India. Perhaps he knows that it is difficult for us to go back now. The children cannot leave their studies, we have our own house and our own jobs over here, and we should never find such good jobs in India.

Yet I am anxious to go back to India for a visit fairly soon if I can manage it. Something my father said when he saw us off at the airport has always stuck in my mind. He said that whenever any relative of his went abroad that was always the last he saw of them. That was the case with both my grandfathers, you will remember. So I always feel that I want to go and visit my parents while they are still alive. They have not seen the baby and I should like them to see him at least once in their lives. But only God can say whether or not this wish of ours will ever by fulfilled.

Part Four

ASHA HAS SOMETHING TO SAY

*

OUR house in India was very nice. It was a big room. We used to sleep and everything in there. Sometimes there were children outside to play with. In India I had a swing, in front of the door. It was in the door, on top of it. Sometimes my Daddy take it off, sometimes he put it up again.

You come up the steps and then there's a room and next door, like a shed. That was our kitchen, where we used to cook our food. My Mummy used to cook our food sitting down on the floor, on a stove, not standing up like in England. There was a little boy called Bikia. He used to come to our kitchen and he used to put his finger through the door to get a *chapatti*. He was nice, very nice. When he come to the kitchen my Mummy put sugar in his mouth. He was a little baby, he lived next door. When we came to England he wrote us a letter that he come to our kitchen and there was no one there, no one gave him sugar and he cried and go back. Really, it was his Daddy wrote the letter. There was just us living up there, and Bikia and his Mummy and Daddy.

I don't know what my teacher's name was in India – she was very old. We didn't call her anything. We just used to go to sleep in that school. My Mummy used to come and fetch me. She didn't go to work in India, just my Daddy. On Sunday we sometimes went out, or we stayed at home and sewed something. My Mum had a machine and I used to watch her while she sewed things. She sewed chair covers for all the chairs in the room. And there were photos all round the walls, of *Babaji*. It was a nice big room with a lock underneath the door. There were trunks by the wall, they were locked. My Mummy kept her ear-rings in them. There were two doors, like that. One was for the kitchen and the other was for the *bera*.

I liked it in the village in India. My aunt used to milk the
buffaloes. She used to give me milk in the cup when she went.
And she had many cows too. We had loads and loads of cows
and some of them died. We had a water tap. It was like a see-
saw. You put the bucket down here and you do this, don't you
– up and down? It was a pump and you can make a see-saw –
sit on it. I didn't get the water out, big ladies used to get it out.
And we used to sit on it and make a see-saw. There was a well
there, too. You have to pull hard to get the water out. But we
had a tap in our house. We had our own cows and our own
tap – in the village, not in Delhi. I liked the village best because
it's much nicer. You can run about more there. There were
some children there. One was my friend. We used to stay a bit
in the village, not much.

When we came here, it was in an aeroplane. It was a big airport. People came to say good-bye, my aunt and uncle and
their children. Then we got on the plane. It was just Mummy,
me, Pritam and Sarinder. What do you call that when you get
sick, and you put something in the bag hanging behind the
seat? The aeroplane people put it and everyone did it in the
bag. But I didn't, I wasn't sick. They gave us sweets to eat on
the aeroplane.

My Daddy came before us and my Daddy was at the airport.
That boy who was at our house last night – his Daddy and my
Daddy came together to get us. Then we went home in the car.
It was someone's car, not ours. We lived in a house near
Mum's work. Then we lived in another house. It was a nice
house, but not the person we lived with, they were not nice. I
don't know why, but they weren't.

Then I started to go to school. When I went to school on the
first day my brother took me, and my Daddy went and told
them my name. Sometimes I cried when I first went to school.
First I was in the nursery class. I did not know English, but
little things I could understand. But some of them not. The
teachers tell me some words. Some of them were nice children.

You know what they do? They come in the morning. When
the bell rings, then everyone goes in. Then the nursery class

play on bicycles and prams and cars. Then there is a play-time and the nursery class play with little horses. It was not the same as our nursery in India. There we used to some go to sleep and some not.

When I went in Class Two I had a nice teacher. Her name was Miss Evans, but I forgot her other name because she changed her name after the holidays. Perhaps she got married. I don't know that. When I went in Class Three she went too. I had a nice time in those two classes. Miss Evans took us to the zoo and oh, what a horrible smell! Such a horrible smell of the animals. The teacher say, 'Our class stay with me, else you get lost.' There were too many people.

I don't like animals much because they smell, but I like hamsters. Miss Evans had a hamster. She cleaned the cage and one day she leave the window open and the cat came in and made the hamster frightened. One day when we were all at home, I think my teacher left the cage open and the hamster got lost in the class room and we found him at the back of the cupboard. But he was died. He was just two years old.

I didn't like school too much when I started going and I don't like it too much even now. The class I am in now, Class Four, there is only one other Indian girl. She is my friend. And another friend lives in my road, the house with the yellow door. She's not Indian, she's English – no, Jamaican. There aren't many Indian children in my school.

In my class a girl says that Asha has got the fever and they don't come near me. But I don't like them either much. Sometimes they hit me and then I go into the boys' playground.

My Indian friend, she is very nice. Her name is Kamla. One day I was feeling sick on the way home from school and I was crying all the way because I was sick. When I got home her Mummy looked after me because my Mummy was still at work. Kamla is my friend but now I don't see her much because she has moved. Two of her brothers and her sister are in India now. I don't know why they are in India. I would like to go to India. I could see Bikia and my aunt's children and the village. But I don't know if I will.

Glossary of Punjabi Words*

anna	a unit of Indian currency. One sixteenth of a *rupee* (q.v.).
Babaji	a term of affectionate respect, used especially to refer to the Sikh saint, Guru Nanak.
Babuji	a term of respect used when addressing an educated person.
Baisakhi	the Hindu spring festival.
Bansi	a low Punjabi caste.
bazar	a shopping centre or market.
ber	a kind of fruit tree.
bera	an enclosed roof terrace.
Bhagvan	God, Lord. This term is often suffixed to the names of certain Hindu deities, e.g. Krishan *Bhagvan*.
Bharvale	a low Punjabi caste.
bidi	a type of crude cigarette sold at most street stalls and stores in India.
Brahman	the Hindu priestly caste.
Chamar	an untouchable caste of tanners and cobblers.

* The purist will note that I have not transliterated from the Gurmukhi spelling system with any consistency, that I have not indicated the relative length of long and short vowels, and that I have used the Roman alphabetical order and not Gurmukhi alphabetical order. I have tried to spell the words in such a way that the English reader may have a rough idea of how they are pronounced, without involving him in a tedious discussion of Punjabi phonetics. Where there are conventional ways of spelling certain words, e.g. *maund, charpoy, tonga,* I have used these for the sake of their familiarity to the reader, even though they may not reflect the Punjabi style of pronouncing these words very accurately.

chapatti	a type of unleavened bread made from wheat flour and baked on a griddle. *Chapatties* and a similar type of bread made from maize flour are major items in the diet of Punjabis and are eaten with vegetables or meat dishes at most meals.
charpoy	the Indian bedstead, strung with rope or webbing and used as an all-purpose item of furniture by poorer Indians.
Chimba	a caste of tailors and washermen.
Chuhra	a low caste of sweepers and scavengers.
dadi	paternal grandmother.
dharamsala	a rest-house for pilgrims and travellers.
dharmbahin	literally 'sister in religion'. Two women who are friendly may contract a kind of fictitious kinship between themselves, usually by participating in some kind of religious ceremony together. They are then said to be *dharmbahin* and ought to treat each other as though they were real sisters.
Divali	the Hindu festival of lights. This feast celebrates the return of the righteous king and hero Rama to his own kingdom after defeating Ravan, the evil king who had kidnapped Rama's wife, Sita.
divankhana	a meeting hall.
Dussehra	a Hindu festival.
Gurmukhi	the script generally used for writing the Punjabi language.
guru	a religious preceptor. The Sikh religion was founded by ten *Gurus*, of whom Nanak was the first.
gurudvara	a Sikh temple. Attached to most *gurudvaras*, both in this country and in India, are rooms which can be used to accommodate anyone in need of shelter. There are many *gurudvaras* in Britain, mainly in the urban areas where large numbers of Sikhs have settled.

hakim	a physician who practises one of the Indian traditional systems of medicine.
Harijans	the name which Gandhi gave to the untouchable castes. Literally, it means 'children of God.'
haveli	house.
havildar, naik, subedar, jemadar	junior ranks in the Indian army.
Hindi	a north Indian language, now the national language of India.
hukka	a water-pipe, or 'hubble-bubble'.
Janam Ashtami or *Krishna Janam Ashtami*	a Hindu festival which commemorates the birth of Krishna, an incarnation of the deity Vishnu. Krishna is supposed to have lived at Brindaban, which is still a popular centre of pilgrimage for his devotees.
Jat	a caste of peasants and farmers, economically and numerically the most important caste in the Punjab.
Jay kerna	literally, to wish someone victory. The phrase is often used to refer to the respectful gesture with folded hands with which Hindus pay homage to a deity.
Julaha	a low caste of weavers.
jutha	impure, polluted. Food left over or defiled by others.
kaccha	In general this term means crude, unfinished, imperfect. When applied to a road it means unsurfaced, or unmetalled. When applied to a house it means clay-built, not faced with stone.
kamiz	a shirt, or a loose dress worn by Punjabi women.
kara	a steel bangle worn by Sikhs as one of the emblems of their religion.
karah	a kind of sweet pudding made from butter, flour and sugar. *Karah* is distributed amongst the congregation in Sikh temples at the end of a service as *prasad* (q.v.).

karma	According to Hindu philosophy, a person is reborn in favourable or unfavourable circumstances according to his *karma*, i.e. the sum total of good or bad works which he has done in his previous birth.
Karol Bagh, *Motiya Khan,* *Pahar Ganj,* *Shish Ganj*	these are streets or districts in Delhi.
kela (plural, *kele*)	banana.
Khatri	a caste of traders and shopkeepers.
kirtan	a religious meeting at which hymns are sung.
laddu	a kind of sweetmeat.
lagan	a part of the Hindu marriage ritual. It precedes the taking of the actual vows and is often held on the evening before the wedding itself.
mahatma	a saintly or holy person.
mandir	a Hindu temple.
maund	a measure of weight, forty *sers* (q.v.).
Mem or *Memsahib*	This term is roughly the equivalent of 'madam' but is often used to refer to a European woman.
Mirasi	a low Punjabi caste.
mohalla	Some large Punjabi villages are divided into several *mohallas,* or wards.
Nai	a caste of barbers.
pakka	complete, finished, cooked, ripe. The opposite of *kaccha*. When applied to a house it means stone-built, or faced with stone.
pan	betel leaf.
panchayat	the council of village elders or representatives which assembles to deal with village affairs and minor offences.
pandit	a learned man, especially a Brahman.

Paramatma	God.
parathas	a kind of bread, something like a thick *chapatti*, shallow fried on a griddle. It can be stuffed with vegetables, or eaten with pickles.
path	a public scripture reading.
pipal	a kind of tree held sacred by Hindus.
Pitaji	a respectful term of reference or address for one's father.
prasad	Any religious meeting among Hindus or Sikhs is concluded with the distribution of sacralised food to all the worshippers. Usually this food consists of some kind of pudding or sweetmeats. It is rather like a communion meal and is thought to convey the blessings of the deity to the congregation. It is known as *prasad* which means, literally, 'grace'.
Punjabi	of the Punjab. The language of the Punjab.
raja	a king.
rupee	a unit of currency. Its value has not been constant over the period dealt with in this book but on the whole it would be safe to reckon that one rupee has generally been the equivalent of about one shilling and sixpence.
Sahib	a term of respect. Sir.
salvar	baggy trousers worn by Punjabi women.
Sanskrit	the Indian classical language.
saran	an inn or rest house attached to a temple.
sari	a kind of dress consisting of five or six yards of cloth draped about the body and tucked into the top of a petticoat at the waist. In the Punjab it is worn mainly by city women, as the village women more usually wear the *salvar-kamiz*.
ser	a measure of weight, roughly equivalent to one kilo.
Sikh	Opinion differs as to whether Sikhism should be regarded as a sect of Hinduism or whether it

should be more properly looked upon as a separate religion. Perhaps it would be accurate to describe it as an offshoot of Hinduism. Sikhism has a philosophy and mode of worship which are not very different from those prevalent among Hindus, but it is more strongly monotheistic and the Sikhs are more highly organised as a religious community than the Hindus.

The Punjab is the homeland of the Sikhs and there are large numbers of both Sikhs and Hindus living in this area. It is sometimes possible to find families where some of the members are Hindus and others are Sikhs, and a certain amount of inter-marriage takes place in some areas.

Sindhi   a person from Sindh. The language of Sindh. Sindh is an area which is now part of Pakistan.

sonf   aniseed.

sucha   pure, uncontaminated. The opposite of *jutha*.

svaga   a game played by small boys in the Punjab.

Teli   a caste of oil pressers.

thanedar   the senior officer in charge of a police station.

tolla   a measure of weight used by goldsmiths.

tonga   a two-wheeled pony carriage which can be hired by the public.

vilayat   abroad; a foreign country, especially England.